"For Makoto Fujimura, caring deeply for souls is a way of life. Through his magnificent paintings, profound essays, and wider leadership with organizations like the National Council on the Arts and the Brehm Center at Fuller Seminary, Fujimura quietly and consistently nurtures artists and the people who love them, both inside and outside the church. In this life-giving book, he cultivates practices that help us honor God by caring for the soul of our culture."

Philip Ryken, president, Wheaton College

"In his generous and inspiring work *Culture Care*, artist Mako Fujimura suggests that our common culture is not a territory to be captured, but a garden to be cultivated, needing the nourishment of creativity, community, connection, and the generation of beauty. It is a grace-filled call to beat swords into plowshares and take up the work of tilling our common garden."

Cherie Harder, president, The Trinity Forum

"What kind of culture do we wish to live within, and how do we get there from here? This is the core question addressed in *Culture Care*, a book suffused with kindness and generosity. It is a book that goes beyond imagination to generation. It suggests and exemplifies ways of being that can help to create well-being. What is the opposite of a vicious cycle—a cycle benevolent, humane, and self-potentiating? We need a term. We need it to name the effect that this wise book can have if we read it, share it, live it."

Robert Schultz, writer, artist, John P. Fishwick Professor of English, Roanoke College

"With much compassion and courage, Makoto compels us to take our calling seriously to care for and cultivate the cultural soil in which we reside. He encourages us to view culture care as a biblical alternative against the prevalent culture of anxiety and scarcity. This is a posture every follower of Jesus should nurture to embody the gospel."

Mark Raja, designer, cofounder of Integrated Arts Movement, Bangalore

"*Culture Care* is a beautiful and powerful work of art, and it is about much more than culture, art, beauty, and aesthetics; it is about nothing less than what it means to be human. We all have a spirit that is thirsty for culture, as do societies at large. This book serves up a powerful warning about what happens when that thirst is not quenched; given the state of the world today, I can only hope that everyone in a leadership position reads, rereads, and ponders what he or she can do to care about culture, and actively so."

John C. Bravman, president, Bucknell University

"The valuable lessons and insights in *Culture Care* are essential to reformation, renewal, hope, and subsequently the restoration of our culture and communities to wholeness. Mako captures what really matters in life: glorifying God in all aspects of our lives and our communities."

Mike Brenan, state president, BB&T, trustee, The Trinity Forum

"While serving with Mako Fujimura on the President's Committee on the Arts and the Humanities, I often experienced his soft-spoken words. When Mako spoke, I wanted to listen because his words brought insight and meaning. The same is true of this book. As I read Mako's words, I listen, allowing them to leave imprints of wisdom on my heart."

Adair Margo, Tom Lea Institute, El Paso, Texas

"My friend Mako Fujimura is one of the most thoughtful, sensitive, and eloquent artists of this generation."

Eric Metaxas, *New York Times* bestselling author of *Bonhoeffer: Pastor, Martyr, Prophet, Spy*

"Mako offers helpful insights not only for artists, but for all partners in culture care. His acknowledgment of the importance of addressing brokenness, creating safe spaces for sharing journeys, and truth telling reflects an appreciation of the relational and transformational power of engaging in culture care. While the reader could be overwhelmed by the pervasiveness of the challenges, Mako inspires us toward meaningful action. A wonderful contribution!"

Alexis Abernethy, professor of psychology, Fuller Theological Seminary

"When I first opened up *Culture Care* one night in Taipei and began reading, I knew that it was an important and essential work for today's artists. As I read, the book kept opening up like a flower of revelation. It helped define for me what I have been doing for a long time: culture care. I never had a word for it before. It has also helped me see myself differently as an artist. *Culture Care* gives the artist dignity and purpose, something that the church and society never gave me. The church never acknowledged art as a worthy vocation with a godly purpose, and society never fully recognized me either. So that's where I've always lived and worked—on the outside. But we are not alone and we are right where we belong!"

James Elaine, artist and curator

"Makoto Fujimura's *Culture Care* is invaluable for a global business leader dealing with multiple cultures and challenging business and cultural decisions every day. I found it to be not only an inspirational reminder to seek beauty in all things, but a practical help in servant leadership."

Carl Chien, MD and head of global investment banking, North Asia, JPMorgan

"Mako Fujimura's words, art, and life all convey an understanding that the common ground of theology and art is our image-bearing humanness—and that an engagement with both our Creator and our creativity are colors that equally belong on the canvas of our culture. His life-giving and rehumanizing summons to culture care fuels the redemptive yearning within each one of us for the world that ought to be."

Matt Heard, author of *Life with a Capital L*

CULTURE CARE

RECONNECTING
WITH BEAUTY FOR
OUR COMMON LIFE

MAKOTO FUJIMURA

FOREWORD BY MARK LABBERTON

IVP Books

An imprint of InterVarsity Press
Downers Grove, Illinois

InterVarsity Press
P.O. Box 1400, Downers Grove, IL 60515-1426
ivpress.com
email@ivpress.com

InterVarsity Press® is the book-publishing division of InterVarsity Christian Fellowship/USA®, a movement of students and faculty active on campus at hundreds of universities, colleges, and schools of nursing in the United States of America, and a member movement of the International Fellowship of Evangelical Students. For information about local and regional activities, visit intervarsity.org.

All Scripture quotations, unless otherwise indicated, are taken from THE HOLY BIBLE, NEW INTERNATIONAL VERSION®, NIV® Copyright © 1973, 1978, 1984, 2011 by Biblica, Inc.™ Used by permission. All rights reserved worldwide.

While any stories in this book are true, some names and identifying information may have been changed to protect the privacy of individuals.

Cover design: David Fassett
Interior design: Dan van Loon
Images: kaleidoscopic: © Yoshinori Kuwahara/Getty Images
plant: © Antonio Trogu/EyeEm/Getty Images
Ki-Seki, © 2014 Makoto Fujimura, mineral pigments, Sumi ink, silver, and gold on Kumohada paper, 60.25 × 45.25 × 1.25 in., private collection.

ISBN 978-0-8308-4503-3 (print)
ISBN 978-0-8308-9111-5 (digital)

Printed in the United States of America ∞

 As a member of the Green Press Initiative, InterVarsity Press is committed to protecting the environment and to the responsible use of natural resources. To learn more, visit greenpressinitiative.org.

Library of Congress Cataloging-in-Publication Data

Names: Fujimura, Makoto, 1960- author.
Title: Culture care : reconnecting with beauty for our common life / Makoto Fujimura ; foreword by Mark Labberton.
Description: Downers Grove : InterVarsity Press, 2017. | Includes bibliographical references.
Identifiers: LCCN 2016046158 (print) | LCCN 2016047996 (ebook) | ISBN 9780830845033 (pbk. : alk. paper) | ISBN 9780830891115 (eBook)
Subjects: LCSH: Fujimura, Makoto, 1960---Ethics. | Fujimura, Makoto, 1960---Philosophy. | Fujimura, Makoto, 1960---Religion. | Art and religion. | Art and philosophy.
Classification: LCC ND237.F79 A35 2017 (print) | LCC ND237.F79 (ebook) | DDC 759.13--dc23
LC record available at https://lccn.loc.gov/2016046158

P	21	20	19	18	17	16	15	14	13	12	11	10	9	8	7	6	5	4	3
Y	34	33	32	31	30	29	28	27	26	25	24	23	22	21	20	19	18

Dedicated to those who sowed seeds of generativity into my life,

starting with Judy and my parents.

CONTENTS

FOREWORD

Mark Labberton

In a world that is at once beautiful and pained, glorious and tortured, thriving and anguished, many ask: Is there hope? What does it look like? Where and what is it?

Hope, first of all, must be realistic. That is, hope can be hope only if it admits that which is darkest while urging toward the light. Nothing glib, or blind, or deflective toward the depth of despair could be a contender for hope. If hope has not first been silenced before the profundity of evil and loss, then such a two-dimensional offering is more scandalous than fruitful. Realistic is not so much concerned with practicality as it is about truthfulness.

Hope also often takes time to mature. On the whole, quick fixes are no match for protracted suffering. Instead, the story of hope is often a long one, with unexpected turns and twists, steps forward and often back too. Time can be both a threat and a friend to hope. Injustice, for example, has to be tediously dismantled, not exploded. This is often infuriating, but it is true. Hope is more like a treatment plan than an adjustment: in other words, hope takes time to shift toward healing.

Hope is disruptive, counter to dominant wind patterns, interrupting what is mapped—a crosscurrent pushing with creativity and truth in directions that many may think neither possible nor desirable. In this sense, when hope arrives, it appears as a longed-for surprise, arriving on some unexpected breeze or with some unanticipated visit.

Hope comes in glimpses, almost never in whole. Needs exist on many levels and in different dimensions, so real hope is unlikely to be present simultaneously for all the needs at hand. And though hope does have starts and critical corners it turns, it is hard to see hope clearly most of the time because no one has sufficient vision to apprehend it all—or even the most critical evidences of its approach. Hope and despair stand close by each other, and yet hope can still seem illusive.

Makoto Fujimura's vision of culture care bears all the marks of an articulate, fully orbed hope and more. Mako's witness to hope is confident but not glib; it's assured but not presumptuous; it's personal but not private. The reason it can be all these things is that Mako's vision of hope centers in the God who holds all reality in the love of Jesus Christ. Nothing and no one is outside the reach of a compassionate and just God.

God, this divine Artist, pays attention to creation in all its reach. God created in freedom and for freedom. Therein lies the great joy alongside the painful sorrow of our human condition. Our troubled and aching world distinctly hopes and suffers in the context of God-marked goodness and of human-marked sin.

Culture care explores the vocation of all humanity, with a particular call on those who seek to attend to our neighbors in God's name. This is the work of all, but most especially artists who see, feel, and embody the story of our beauty and our suffering, our longing, anger, pain, and hope.

Artists, those whom Mako calls "border-stalkers," live and work at the edge, on the margins of the social mainstream where they contribute powerful insights, alarms, reflections, and yearnings about our human situation. Their work establishes the urgency of the arts as honest and courageous testimonies of suffering and hope. Artists who do this work because of the generative influence of their Christian faith can be wellsprings of honesty and courage in these vital tasks.

Mako's encompassing vision of culture care grips our imagination, stimulates our hope, and enlarges our longing for a world renewed by the reality of God's light and love. This is the work of the church into today's context. Whether inside or outside the bounds of a sanctuary or congregation, culture care is our vocation and mission.

Mako's role at Fuller Theological Seminary as director of the Brehm Center for Worship, Theology, and the Arts is an invaluable, necessary gift for us at Fuller to accomplish our goal of forming global leaders for kingdom vocations. How could such transformative work be undertaken without the arts? Without that fundamental affirmation and practice of creative imagination in action? This is what's needed to live out the call of God in all the times and places into which our faculty and alumni will scatter in Christ's name.

Culture care is the imaginative effluence of being a faithful follower of Jesus in any time or place. It's hope borne into places where hope that is truly hope must be realistic, slow, disruptive, and limited. Mako's encompassing, inspiring, humble, bold vision is life giving because it is what life is meant to be. Culture care is needed everywhere.

PREFACE

*T*his is a book for artists, but artists come in many forms. Anyone with a calling to create—from visual artists, musicians, writers, and actors to entrepreneurs, pastors, and business professionals—will resonate with its message. This book is for anyone who feels the cultural divide, especially those with a desire or an artistic gift to reach across boundaries with understanding, reconciliation, and healing. It is a book for anyone with a passion for the arts, for supporters of the arts, and for creative catalysts who understand how much the culture we all share affects human thriving today and shapes the generations to come.

Culture care, though a thesis I have developed, is a movement already afoot in culture in various circles. In one sense this book is not new or unique; International Arts Movement, the Fujimura Institute, and the Brehm Center are part of a whole ecosystem of a greater movement. But having acknowledged that, this is a book that addresses head-on a terrible rift in our society: our culture is given the hope of restoration and the new creation to come. Like the creation care movement that looks after the environment and the soul care concepts provided by practitioners in mental health and spiritual growth, this book on culture care lays out a necessary conceptual framework and the beginnings of practical responses to repair the rift. This is a book meant to inspire individuals and to inform the wider movement in providing care, for us to become co-makers with the divine Artist into the new creation.

Since the publication of my small booklet called *On Becoming Generative: An Introduction to Culture Care* (included with minor adaptations here), much has already happened in public conversations about culture. While working on this book I met with James Davison Hunter, a sociologist widely known for his groundbreaking work on the American culture wars, at the University of Virginia's Institute for Advanced Studies in Culture. Hunter affirmed this journey toward culture care, noting that poetry (and the arts in general) and generative thinking are critical for our society to begin a shift away from our corrosive culture battles.

While I base my thinking and applications on a Christian perspective and often work with people within Christian communities, this thesis is not limited to Christians. The principles of culture care can be embraced universally. They depend only on developing skills in listening to the wider culture, and thereby becoming a loving servant toward culture rather than treating it as territory to be won.

Some people may find what I term a Christian perspective debatable, nebulous, meaningless, or even offensive, but I dare to suggest that this book may be helpful even for such people. As I will explain, my thesis, flowing out of my pilgrimage with Jesus of Nazareth, has led me into a wider journey, discovering my role as a "border-stalker" and moving in and out of arts institutions, churches, and other organizations. I write this from the margins of all these diverse forms of infrastructure, hoping to speak into the hearts of all those who desire to seek the truth and fill the world again with beauty.

Two words of thanks: the initial spark that led to the coinage of the term "culture care" came from my friend and executive editor Caleb Seeling. It was in a car, on a winding road to the Aspen Institute, that he suggested I consider writing this book. Thanks also to Mark Rodgers and Amy Jones of the Wedgwood Circle for initiating the printing of the first culture care booklet, which has garnered so much attention.

1

ON BECOMING GENERATIVE

BRINGING BEAUTY INTO OUR LIVES

*A*s a newlywed couple, my wife and I began our journey with very little. After Judy and I got married in the summer of 1983, after college, we moved to Connecticut for Judy to pursue her master's degree in marriage counseling. I taught at a special education school and painted at home. We had a tight budget and often had to ration our food (lots of tuna cans!) just to get through the week.

One evening I was sitting alone, waiting for Judy to come home to our small apartment, worried about how we were going to afford the rent and pay for necessities over the weekend. Our refrigerator was empty and I had no cash left.

Then Judy walked in, and she had brought home a bouquet of flowers. I got really upset.

"How could you think of buying flowers if we can't even eat!" I remember saying, frustrated.

Judy's reply has been etched in my heart for over thirty years now. *"We need to feed our souls, too."*

The irony is that I am an artist. I am the one, supposedly, feeding people's souls. But in worrying for tomorrow, in the stoic responsibility

I felt to make ends meet, to survive, I failed to be the artist. Judy was the artist: she brought home a bouquet.

I do not remember what we ended up eating that day, or that month (probably tuna fish). But I do remember that particular bouquet of flowers. I painted them.

"We *need* to feed our souls, too." Those words still resonate with me today.

Is Judy still right? Do we, as human beings, need more than food and shelter? Do we need beauty in our lives? Given our limited resources, how do we cultivate and care for our souls? And how do these questions apply to the larger culture?

My life as an artist, and as a founder of International Arts Movement (IAM), has been in pursuit of questions like these—not just internally or for my own sake but with a growing global network of people. What began as an admission of my own failure to be an artist has now given birth to many principles that govern my life as an artist, father, husband, and leader. I call them generative principles. What started out as Judy's care for our own souls has blossomed into an effort to extend that care into our home and our churches, and into a vision for culture at large. What I call culture care is a generative approach to culture that brings bouquets of flowers into a culture bereft of beauty.

AN ARTIST'S JOURNEY TOWARD GENERATIVITY

I have found that what I am asked to do often seems impossible. How can I make a living as an artist? How can I support my family as an artist? How can I support a growing movement as an artist? These challenges seem to expand with every opportunity, but in my mind they come back to the same generative principles.

This book launches a series of essays and conversations on culture care, to which I invite the contributions of artists, curators, critics, patrons, and other lovers of the arts and participants in culture. We anticipate more books on culture care, and the theological underpinning for my thesis will be laid out in my upcoming book on a theology of making. To help frame the conversation for different types of thinkers, I begin by briefly considering three G's sparked by Judy's act that have come to characterize my approach to generative thinking:

- genesis moments

- generosity

- generational thinking

In the next chapter, I will draw these elements together with more formal definitions of the terms *generative* and *culture care* to help shape and catalyze an ongoing conversation.

ᗧ ᗧ ᗧ

Bringing home a bouquet of flowers created a *genesis moment* for me. Judy's small act fed my soul. It renewed my conviction as an artist. It gave me new perspective. It challenged me to deliberately focus on endeavors in which I could truly be an artist of the soul. That moment engendered many more genesis moments in the years that followed, contributing to decisions small and large that have redefined my life and provided inspiration for myself, my family, and my communities.

Genesis moments like this often include elements of the great story told in the beginning of the biblical book of Genesis: creativity, growth—and failure. Two of these elements are common in discussions about arts and culture. God creates and calls his creatures to fruitfulness. Adam exercises his own creativity in naming what has been created. But the story also runs into failure and finitude.

Generative thinking often starts out with a failure, like my failure to think and act as an artist. I have discovered that something is awakened through failure, tragedy, and disappointment. It is a place of learning and potential creativity. In such moments you can get lost in despair or denial, or you can recognize the failure and run toward the hope of something new.

The key to recognizing genesis moments is to assume that every moment is fresh. Creativity applied in a moment of weakness and vulnerability can turn failure into enduring conversation, opening new vistas of inspiration and incarnation. To remember what Judy did, to speak of it with others, to value her care—all this is generative, as her act can be honored and become a touchpoint for others, leading to the birth of ideas and actions, artifacts and relationships that would not otherwise have been.

ꙮ ꙮ ꙮ

The bouquet was also an emblem of *generosity*. Judy's generous heart—more generous than mine at that moment—valued beauty over the day-to-day worries that had so nearly narrowed my focus. Generative thinking is fueled by generosity because it so often must work against a mindset that has survival and utility in the foreground. In a culture dominated by this mindset, generosity has an unexpectedness that can set the context for the renewal of our hearts. An encounter with generosity can remind us that life always overflows our attempts to reduce it to a commodity or a transaction—because it is a gift. Life and beauty are gratuitous in the best senses of that word.

Judy's bouquet is only one of many instances of generosity in my life. I was able to become an artist partly because of my parents' generosity and encouragement. Both my father and my mother encouraged me when I desired to pursue the arts. That, for an Asian family, was extremely unusual. Music, painting, writing, and creating have always been part of my life. I took them for granted and thought that everyone's homes were a nurturing environment for creativity. Then I went to middle school and discovered I was an anomaly! It was then that I started to realize I somehow had to defend my time for creativity in a culture that does not nurture creative growth.

Artists have a deep capacity to develop and share generosity and empathy, to point toward abundance and connections. We learn generosity as we try to communicate with a new audience, or help people express what they cannot otherwise articulate, or say something meaningful into the void. Even an artist who journeys alone, like the poet Emily Dickinson, can develop a sense of communicating or communing with someone—the reader, nature, God—and so strengthen critical generative capacities to bring beauty into the world. An encounter with the arts can lead to generative thinking as generosity supplants our quid pro quo expectations. (In the sciences too discovery is linked to the generosity of information shared among its practitioners.) The effects of generosity begin with gratitude and lead to places we cannot predict.

𝕺 𝕺 𝕺

As I reflect on Judy's simple act and on my life in the arts, I am more and more convinced that anything truly generative is not isolated. Generative values are given to us as a gift by our parents and predecessors. They grow in conversation with the past and in our intention to speak and create so as to cultivate the values of multiple future generations. Generative thinking requires *generational thinking*.

Culture formation is generational, not birthed in a night. Generative thinking can inspire us to work within a vision for culture that is expressed in centuries and millennia rather than quarters, seasons, or fashions. People in the arts work in conversation with artists of the past as they are shaping the future, attempting to produce work with enduring qualities that might in turn speak to new generations.

I have seen gratuitous acts modeled by Judy's parents and family. I have failed at times to appreciate my own parents' generosity—but at least I have had the receptivity to repent! My father's generosity in particular has led to so many blessings in the world that he did not expect or even realize—all flowing from his love for art and music. Such acts from Judy's and my parents are now reflected in unexpected ways, not least in the lives of our creative children, all of whom deeply value beauty and model generosity.

Even the term *generative* is a gift to me. My father, Osamu Fujimura, is a pioneer of acoustics research. I was born in Boston because he was doing postdoctoral research at MIT with Noam Chomsky. Recently I invited my father to attend an International Arts Movement conference. As we walked together to the TriBeCa Performance Center where I was about to give a keynote, he asked me what I was to speak on. I told him the speech would be called "On Generative Culture." My father responded, "Interesting . . . the word *generative* . . . that was my thesis topic."

I knew that. I had even read the thesis. But for some reason I had sidelined this influence and forgotten to link my theme to my father's lifetime of work! He was instrumental in bringing Chomsky's Generative Grammar Theory to Japan. I was grateful for the rediscovery and was able to present my version of generative thinking with a proper attribution of his influence.

Our lives are directed or constrained by paths paved by the generations before us. Sometimes we can trace the paths, as I did with my father. Often they shape us unawares. What is true of legacies from our parents is true also for our communities and racial and national histories. Cultures are not created overnight. We are affected by layers of experiences, personalities, and works of previous generations. Cultural histories affect us far beyond what we are able to recognize—or, sometimes, admit.

Generative principles flow out of generational blessing toward creativity. But the positive examples of my wife and my parents are all too rare. Many people look back on what can seem to be generational curses rather than blessings. I created IAM and continue to advocate for the arts from a conviction that all people need a place of nurture toward their creative growth. Acts of generosity can inspire genesis moments even out of generational failures.

✑ ✑ ✑

This book is the first in a series on culture care that will expand on these and other generative principles and apply them to several cases. It is my hope to engender conversations and so gather a community of people committed to generative living. This, it should be emphasized, is not an end in itself but a contribution to the greater good. Generative paths will birth resourcefulness, patience, and general creativity in all of life. They lead to cultural—and human—thriving.

2

CULTURE CARE DEFINED

*C*ulture care is to provide care for our culture's "soul," to bring to our cultural home our bouquet of flowers so that reminders of beauty—both ephemeral and enduring—are present in even the harshest environments where survival is at stake. We may need to learn to cultivate these reminders of beauty in the same way flowers are cared for and raised. Culture care restores beauty as a seed of invigoration into the ecosystem of culture. Such care is generative: a well-nurtured culture becomes an environment in which people and creativity thrive.

At this point it will be helpful to gather the threads to find a working definition of my main terms. At the most basic level, we call something *generative* if it is fruitful, originating new life or producing offspring (as with plants and animals), or producing new parts (as with stem cells). When we are generative, we draw on creativity to bring into being something fresh and life giving.

We can also approach generativity by looking at its shadow, *degenerate*, the loss of good or desirable qualities (a term also frequently used of generations). What is generative is the opposite of degrading or limiting. It is constructive, expansive, affirming, growing beyond a mindset of scarcity.

One of Noam Chomsky's early definitions of "generative grammar" refers to the set of rules that can be used to create or generate all grammatical sentences in a language.[1] He was looking in human languages, as did my father in his work in acoustics, for a universal generative principle, an explanation of our ability to construct seemingly infinite phrases by switching out elements from a finite vocabulary and grammatical framework. Building on this, we might say that a generative approach will identify and model the "grammar" or conditions that best contribute to a good life and a thriving culture.

Discovering and naming this grammar, identifying and then living truly generative principles, is a process that depends deeply on generosity. This is because it requires us to open ourselves to deep questions (and to their answers), which is impossible when survival seems to depend on competing for scarce resources. But when we acknowledge the gratuitous nature of life—not least the world's inordinately diverse beauty—gratitude galvanizes us to ask and welcome questions that reach beyond our own context and experience. Artists at their best help us with such questions by presenting an expansive vision of life that reveals beauty in ever-wider zones.

Such a vision is by its nature a challenge to dictators and totalitarian regimes—a threat to those whose power depends on holding humanity at the level of survival or, worse, on eliminating diverse elements from societies. Artists and other generative people can sense dehumanizing trends quickly, and this is why they are often targeted by autocrats. But artists ultimately can reveal new facets of human flourishing even in the midst of tragedy or horror, pointing toward hope and meaning.

Another key generative principle emerges as we begin to escape the cramped thinking of a culture of scarcity: stewardship. Beyond mere survival, job function, bureaucratic specialization, or social roles is a wide scope of human concern and responsibility. We are all given gifts for which we all must care. Just as we are learning the importance of taking care of our environment to leave the earth healthy for future generations, so we must all care for culture so future generations can thrive.

Implied in this description is a measure by which to assess principles that claim to be generative: thinking and living that are truly generative make possible works and movements that make our culture more humane and welcoming and that inspire us to be more fully human. We can be comfortable, even confident, in affirming a cultural contribution as generative if, over time, it recognizes, produces, or catalyzes more beauty, goodness, and flourishing.

What emerges from generative moments is something new, transformed from its source, something that is both free and responsible to make its own ongoing creative contribution. I have on my farm a magnificent old pear tree. This tree has grown from a small seed. First, the seed died. It found welcoming soil and morphed into a tiny shoot. In time, with nurture, it came to full growth, a thing of beauty at many levels, all on a scale out of proportion to the original seed, and full of generative potential in its turn. The tree provides shade and shelter, flowers and fruit. It might provide wood for warmth or walls or works of art. It might contribute to a landscape or resist erosion. It might inspire poems or plays, paintings or photographs (such as the *Ki-Seki* painting at the front of this book). It might spark a scientific discovery, host children at play, or lead a man or woman to reflect on the nature of life.

We can say that culture care is applied generative thinking. Culture care ultimately results in a generative cultural environment: open to questions of meaning, reaching beyond mere survival, inspiring people to meaningful action, and leading toward wholeness and harmony. It produces thriving crossgenerational community.

INTERLUDE: WHEN BEAUTY WAS TABOO

By intentionally using the word *beauty*, I am swimming upstream. When I began to exhibit in New York City in the mid-1990s, "beauty" was taboo, not to be spoken of in public. It signified cultural hegemony, imperialist power, the corruption of the past, or the cosmetic sheen of superficial contemporary culture. The art world still resists this word.

The first time I spoke at Dillon Gallery in SoHo, I quoted the text of Isaiah 61:2-3:

> to comfort all who mourn,
>   and provide for those who grieve in Zion—
> to bestow on them a crown of beauty
>   instead of ashes,
> the oil of joy
>   instead of mourning,
> and a garment of praise
>   instead of a spirit of despair.

At times in my own journey, even long after Judy's reminder of a bouquet of flowers, I have struggled to incorporate beauty into my life. As a National Scholar graduate student in Japan, studying the art of Nihonga, I found myself using such extravagantly beautiful materials as gold, silver, malachite, azurite, and exquisite paper and silk. I wrestled with beauty revealed in front of me, created with my own hands. I did not then have a conceptual framework to incorporate beauty as a valid premise of contemporary art. At that first artist's talk at Dillon Gallery, I spoke of this struggle and how, on finding the central reality of Jesus Christ, I was for the first time able to find in Christ himself an integrating premise behind beauty.

For Christ also began his ministry with a reading from Isaiah 61.

The Spirit of the Lord is on me,
    because he has anointed me
    to proclaim good news to the poor.
He has sent me to proclaim freedom for the prisoners
    and recovery of sight for the blind,
to set the oppressed free. (Luke 4:18)

Then he shocked those in the audience by claiming, "Today this scripture is fulfilled in your hearing" (Luke 4:21). Jesus of Nazareth claimed to be the one who can provide for us a "crown of beauty instead of ashes." He claimed to be the source of this beauty.

In mentioning beauty—let alone Christ—in a room filled with people of the art world, I knew that I was transgressing against what was culturally acceptable for them. But as his follower, I needed to acknowledge Christ's claims, to hold them up in this public sphere as something we can test. I wanted to begin to reclaim beauty and to frame it for our time as a gift given to us by the Creator. I wanted to help recover a view of beauty as a gift that we discover, receive, and steward.

The next day, a critic who had been in the audience called and surprised me by saying, "I have never heard anybody quote Isaiah in the art world and mean it with conviction. I was moved by what you had to say." Thus began a journey to create and present beauty in the harsh and cynical environment of the New York art world.

WORKING ASSUMPTIONS

The framework of culture care rests on a number of foundational assumptions. Many resemble what one might expect when applying the principles of environmental stewardship (known in some circles as creation care) to cultural stewardship. I am assuming that efforts to restore the cultural environment are good and noble and that our efforts will benefit the next generation. I am assuming that an attempt to speak with people through conversations and questions that are outside the current cultural and ideological divide is healthy and will ultimately help culture thrive. In a polarized cultural reality that causes culture wars, even such assumptions may be challenged. The paralysis stemming from culture wars has decimated the fundamental trust in "the other," and we are unable to move beyond the conflict. A culture care stance brings in, despite this reality, a fresh new start, as culture care focuses on the promise of new creation, the potential of new types of communities.

As an artist and a Christian, I find the source and goal of beauty, of generative thinking, and of responsible action in the biblical understanding of what our lives are for. We find our creative identity in God. Genesis moments can be assumed simply because God is the great Artist, and we are God's artists, called to steward the creation entrusted to our care. The good news of the Bible is that in Christ we are journeying toward ultimate wholeness, integration, and well-being. We are becoming more fully what we were made to be, to the benefit of all creation.

But culture care and generative principles are not concepts only for Christian believers or churches or religious conversations. *Culture care is everyone's business.* Everyone can—and I gratefully acknowledge that many people from all sorts of backgrounds do—contribute to the common good. These conversations are open to all people of good will. To make culture inhabitable, to make it a place of nurture for creativity, we must all choose to give away beauty gratuitously.

Gratuitous can be a negative word, as in "gratuitous violence," but here I am using it to speak of intentionality, and even forcefulness, which, as we will see in later chapters, is necessary in our deeply fragmented culture. I will also be looking at how the reality of beauty can help integrate such fragmentation.

3

BLACK RIVER, CRACKED LANDS

*P*eople in Western cultures often think of themselves first as individuals, but the human being may be better understood as a focal point of embedded relationships. Sometimes we are more aware of our dependence and sometimes we are more aware of our contributions, but we exist in community—in families, in places. In churches and work groups. In economies and ecologies. What is more, our multifaceted interactions with our physical and cultural environment directly affect our bodies, our minds, our spirits, and ultimately our souls.

We can talk about all these elements separately, but we cannot actually isolate our reactions (much as we might like to). Any experience that affects our relationships affects our minds, which affects our bodies, and so on, back and forth. If we are to thrive, we can do so only as part of a wider, interrelated ecosystem. Thriving ecosystems are known for abundance and diversity, hospitable even to those who want to dwell as outliers and remain on the margins.

Judy reminded us that our souls need food as well as our bodies. We will discuss how beauty feeds the soul in a later chapter, but first we should address the related issue of the consequences when the soul is starved. What happens to communities when our souls are fed from the produce of a polluted ecosystem? This is the situation in which we live today. We need to be aware of the greater cultural reality that is causing this imbalance so that we can find the best path toward culture care.

An industrial map in the mid-twentieth century colored New York's Hudson River black. The mapmakers considered a black river a good thing—full of industry! The more factory outputs, the more progress. When that map was made, "nature" was widely seen as a resource to be exploited. Few people considered the consequences of careless disposal of industrial waste. The culture has shifted dramatically over the last fifty years. When I share this story today, most people shudder and ask how anyone could think of a polluted river as good.

But today we are doing the same thing with the river of culture. Think of the arts and other cultural enterprises as rivers that water the soil of culture. We are painting this cultural river black—full of industry, dominated by commercial interests, careless of toxic by-products—and there are still cultural mapmakers who claim that this is a good thing. The pollution makes it difficult for us to breathe, difficult for artists to create, difficult for any of us to see beauty through the murk.

It is widely recognized that our culture today is not life giving. There is little room at the margins to make artistic endeavors sustainable. The wider ecosystem of art and culture has been decimated, leaving only homogeneous pockets of survivors, those fit enough to survive in a poisoned environment. In culture as in nature, a lack of diversity is a first sign of a distressed ecosystem.

Many of the streams that feed the river of culture are polluted, and the soil this river should be watering is thus parched and fragmented.

Most of these examples are well-known, but let me briefly touch on some of the fault lines in the cultural soil (starving the soul) as well as some of the sources of the poisons in the water (polluting the soul).

STARVING THE CULTURAL SOUL

One of the most powerful sources of cultural fragmentation has grown out of the great successes of the Industrial Revolution. Its vision, standards, and methods soon proliferated beyond the factory and the economic realm and were embraced in sectors from education to government and even church. The result was reductionism. Modern people began to equate progress with efficiency. Despite valiant and ongoing resistance from many quarters—including within industry—success for a large part of our culture is now judged by efficient production and mass consumption. We often value repetitive, machine-like performance as critical to bottom-line success. In the seductive industrialist mentality, people become "workers" or "human resources" who are first seen as interchangeable cogs, then treated as machines—and are now often replaced by machines.

A related cultural fault line is hyperspecialization, where a person or firm focuses on increasingly narrow segments of a production process, discipline, artistic genre, or market. One result is an increasing prominence in our culture of the "expert." The expert knows one part, not the whole, and often not even the wider field in which they work. They consciously reduce their scope of concern to go deeper in their discipline. But increased clarity on a narrow point usually comes at the price of blindness to context and to one's working assumptions. It often brings isolation from—and sometimes alienation from or hostility to—those with differing expertise.

Today's expert usually shies away from questions of meaning and connection and responsibility—referring such issues to those who "specialize" in meaning. This is, of course, fundamentally unsatisfying for human beings and contributes to our cultural unease. It also has troubling consequences within a discipline. My father's career offers an example of this.[1]

☙ ☙ ☙

My father spent years at Tokyo University after his research with Chomsky, and he later joined the famed Bell Laboratories pure-research complex in Murray Hill, New Jersey. It was at Bell Labs in the early 1970s that he began to notice fundamental deficiencies in acoustics research. In the 1980s, in his early fifties, my father began to send a series of notes to his colleagues questioning basic tenets of their field. He found many of their approaches flawed because they were based on reductionist assumptions. They did not fit the data and were thus inadequate and unable to reach their stated goals.

In my simplified understanding, the early research assumed that you could generate enough data to rebuild speech by segmenting speech patterns. It seems a bit like dissecting a frog and stitching it back together, only to expect it to jump again—a typical modernist approach. Researchers expected to be able to simulate natural-sounding human speech within a decade, and they predicted the rise of technologies like Apple's Siri and Google's voice navigation. But my father was right. Even the best such technologies thirty years later sound choppy and machine-like.

Though he was dealing with a community of scientists—who are supposed to be known for their mental flexibility—it took years before my father could present his new ideas to the linguistics/phonetics community. Many tenured professors, I am sure, found his claims threatening to their assumptions. Prior to this time my father had never had problems finding support for his research, such as government grants, but now he found himself fighting the research establishment that he had himself helped to build. After many futile attempts to secure funding, my brother, a successful Silicon Valley entrepreneur, stepped in to fund a post for a graduate student to help my father compile enough data to begin his research.

That today's computer voices sound as good as they do is in part the result of my father's work. After the breakup of AT&T in the 1980s, he spent many years at Ohio State trying to introduce a new path called C/D (Converter/Distributor) theory. This theory is not so much concerned with segmenting language as with recognizing patterns of vocal stress and intonation. He calls this approach *prosodic*, as it better accounts for the natural complexity of speech and language.

ᴓ ᴓ ᴓ

Most of us recognize the shortcomings of reductionism at a deep level: we know that we are more than what we produce and that efficiency is not the point of education, religion, art, play, or many other aspects of human culture. Most people are dissatisfied with the reductionist viewpoint, yet not enough of us have or can articulate viable alternatives because reductionism has taken over not only how people define success but also what we value in society. Many in our culture no longer value a bouquet of flowers because beauty contributes neither to the machinery of production nor to an advantage in the latest cultural battle—and because the pressure for continued consumption warps our capacity to appreciate and enjoy.

It is not the desire to survive or to provide for a family that is problematic. Cultural fragmentation comes rather when we fall into the trap of treating survival as the bottom line and thus neglect the holistic approaches that demand personal growth and point our civilization toward a greater vision. Fragmentation comes when we forget the importance of beauty for our lives and the necessity—for both individual and social flourishing—of sharing the experience of beauty in community.

In the face of reductionism, we must recall that human beings are not "human doings," as one of my mentors says.[2] We are more than animals following our instincts to compete and survive. Human culture encompasses more than loyalty to a den, herd, or pack. Our concern as individuals and families should thus be to raise, educate, and form whole persons—to cultivate connected citizens who can co-create thriving communities, cities, and nations.

POLLUTING THE CULTURAL SOUL

I see the fragmentation and reductionism operating in culture today as releasing two main pollutants into the river of culture. They are what I call *overcommodification of art* and *utilitarian pragmatism*. Today, instead of regarding art as a visionary gift to society we see it as a means for commercial gain. Those artists who aspire to anything other than market success are often caught up in the culture wars, their works put to use as ideological tools—or weapons—in those divisive struggles. These pollutants are choking the creatures that should be swimming and contributing to the diversity of expression.

Reductionism is no stranger to the arts. What my father experienced as a scientist in battling against reductionism, artists were experiencing very early in the twentieth century. In culture, reductionism grew not from a rational path toward specialization but in response to the impending threat of humanity's weapons used against ourselves. In the aftermath of two world wars, artists began to articulate the culture's dramatic loss of humanity. For many, Hiroshima and Nagasaki revealed the naiveté of earlier attempts to capture beauty via canvas or concert hall. In movements such as Dadaism and abstract expressionism, artists created images that visualized trauma, disillusionment, and dehumanization and attempted to counter it not with beauty but with irony or the pure power of expressive gestures. The resulting work, an honest depiction of our loss, screams at us with contempt for a dehumanized view of life.

At the same time, artists recognized the gap left by the weakening witness of the church in culture and increasingly came to see themselves as secular prophets and priests with a call to speak the truth against the establishment. They intentionally isolated themselves from society and produced work aimed at shocking people into recognizing and decrying the horrors of the age. As critic Robert Hughes has noted, "the shock of the new" became a way of life in the twentieth-century modernist experiment.[3]

Artists such as Marcel Duchamp, Mark Rothko, and Ad Reinhardt point to a world in which art is no longer decoration or representation of historical events. By creating a new language with which to speak into society, they began to express an artistic via negativa—a version of the Christian theological and philosophical tradition that points to truth by emphasizing what truth is not. These artists created an aesthetic antithesis to the direct linkage of art and power (Duchamp), depicted the angst of the "edge" of our time and space (Rothko), and pursued the purity of sensory experiences to see beyond representation (Reinhardt).

During this period the voices of artists became more and more esoteric and elitist. Their work was generative, providing ways for viewers to confront the dehumanized world. But at the same time, a reductionist vision began to solidify (especially among the critics), so that artists' confrontational nature and insistence on defining themselves against the status quo resulted only in ideological fragmentation and marginalization. Even the new ideals that they had for art—for the purity and unity of expression—made little contact with the lives of most people in their culture.

The gap between artists and the wider society has only widened since the rise of the culture wars and the increasingly overt use of art in that struggle. All artists have been conscripted by progressive draft boards as frontline soldiers to defend "freedom of expression" against tradition and conformity. It is a disturbing irony that freedom of expression and the diversity of artistic voices have been early casualties. Artists have been pressed—sometimes willingly and sometimes not—to speak not for their own work, vision, and principles but for (usually leftist) ideologies. The implicit and explicit cultural pressures toward ideological uniformity are so high that one could say that in the culture wars artists are free to express anything *other* than beauty.

As the ideals faded, what was left was commercialism. Think of Andy Warhol's pop art featuring Marilyn Monroe and Campbell's soup cans. He was brilliant in capturing the icons of his age with an exquisite touch and personal flair. But though his own works were generative, providing an important conversation and an enduring legacy, his pop art led to thousands of derivative works, flooding the market. With the exception of ideological uses, today's art has been commoditized to such an extent that we often see commerce as the prevailing goal of art and value the arts only as transactional tools to achieve fame and thus wealth.

The shock of the new has devolved to a game of gaining the fifteen minutes of fame that Warhol forecast each of us will someday have. In our river metaphor, the artists are struggling in polluted waters to find the oxygen they need to create. Artists are adaptable, but surviving in a stressed ecosystem like ours often means becoming bottom-feeders like catfish, feeding off the lowest layers of culture, and the pollution there turns many into monstrous, hideous creatures. Their creativity is given over to survival—and those who are fittest to survive are usually those who fashion the cleverest means to twist and adapt to the celebrity model of art. Too often they create primarily what they think will sell. Speaking recently to a group of musicians, I implored them not to do so. "Be a trout instead," I said. "Endeavor to go upstream into the tributaries and find clear, pure waters. Create upstream, and then what you create will affect the whole stream."

But the problem for them, and for me, is that today no pure waters are to be found upstream either. Thus a key culture care strategy, as we will see later, is to create diverse microcosms of pure water so that "trout" can survive in our cultural ecosystem.

෨ ෨ ෨

We are living in a time of cultural upheaval. No matter what field an artist operates in, the sustainability of art that points us beyond ourselves is threatened. Every sphere is being shaken up. Galleries have faced a frozen market since the Lehman shock of 2008. Every midtier gallery in New York's Chelsea neighborhood now struggles to pay rent. The music industry is no longer able to give lucrative contracts to musicians because every song is now worth 99 cents. Top modern dancers have to pay for rehearsal space out of their own pockets. Publishers, threatened by the lower margins of Amazon sales and electronic books, are offering less and less rewarding contracts to writers. Even established first-rate writers cannot count on being given a New York City reading today because it is not worth the risk for the publisher.

We could be facing a public eclipse of those species called art, dance, and music. (Poetry is the only field that seems to be producing at a terrific pace at the moment, partly because poets do not depend on commercial forces to keep writing. But not many of us seem to be *reading* poetry.) The arts audience is changing and shrinking amid an ever-demanding chorus of offers online that change how we assess the value of an experience.

Why is culture care needed? From the perspective of the arts, it is because today an artist cannot simply paint; a novelist cannot simply write; a pianist cannot simply play. Utilitarian pragmatism and commercialism so thoroughly pervade culture that without some shift in worldview and expectation, what we do as artists—the activities of the arts—will be neither sustainable nor generative. We will not be able to resist their use as weapons in the culture wars.

We need to recognize our time as a genesis moment.

4

FROM CULTURE WARS
TO A COMMON LIFE

*T*he cultural fragmentation we have experienced, and the reductionism that has accompanied minute categorization within all disciplines, has contributed directly to today's polarized ideological positions. Too many of us live isolated—sometimes more literally, sometimes virtually—with the tribes on our own cultural islands. We have no meaningful engagement with or understanding of the human beings across the divide. Few people are able or willing to build bridges. When we are living in a mode of survival and scarcity rather than generativity, we easily fall into viewing those outside as enemies locked in utter competition for commodities or power that should be ours.

Sociologist James Davison Hunter noted more than twenty years ago that participants in culture wars employ language that reduces the "enemy" to a caricature, portraying their ideas as not only false but pernicious, alienating their humanity. Hunter identifies the culprit in *Culture Wars*, arguing that a shared weakness "in both orthodox and progressivist alliances" is "an implicit yet imperious disregard for the goal of a *common life*."[1]

This "disregard for the goal of a common life" is the abject failure of our times. Yet from this failure we can begin a new path toward culture care.

Culture is not a territory to be won or lost but a resource we are called to steward with care. *Culture is a garden to be cultivated.*

I have seen this type of care modeled. From 2003 to 2009 I served on the National Council on the Arts, advising National Endowment for the Arts chair Dana Gioia. He often stated that "the NEA is the Poland of the culture wars: everyone wants to fight on her turf, but no one cares about her inhabitants." Gioia, who is one of the leading poets in the United States, had also been a business executive. His approach to culture drew from both standpoints, and it included bringing disciplined management to the agency. While I served on the Council I saw him work diligently to build consensus around caring for our culture. I saw that it is possible for a political leader in Washington to work toward the common good.

But all too often politicians and political factions take an easier path, picking on the arts as instigators of cultural ills. Few make the effort to care for culture. Few acknowledge in artists the potential and opportunity to help us express our deepest longings for a free and humane society.

After many years of culture wars, no one can claim victory. We have all been further dehumanized, fragmented, and exiled from genuine conversation. Culture at large is a polluted, overcommoditized system that has failed all of us.

Certainly ideas are worth defending and fighting for, but we have now come to a point where even the core principles of contemporary ideologies have been compromised. The language of both liberalism and conservatism has been truncated and distorted, and this dysfunction is dismantling the language of culture. We need mediation in culture to help bridge the divide—not so much to broker an agreement about what we believe as to communicate beyond our differences.

❁ ❁ ❁

Is there an alternative to the ongoing starvation or pollution of our cultural soul? How can we step back from a utilitarian or commercial posture toward the arts and culture? When we commit to culture care, one of the things we commit to is moving beyond poisoned language and the "imperious disregard" for the life of those unlike ourselves that Hunter notes. Culture care emphasizes the common good.

Constructive cultural work begins not in opposition but in sharing—of ideals generously argued, of visions for future generations, of opportunities to meet and dialogue with the other—all of which could occur in the context of the arts and from there be mirrored into society. From this point culture care can and will lead to rigorous debate—debate that is aimed not at defending homogeneous ideological tribes but at ways to care for the whole of culture and all of its participants.

With this approach we can perhaps redeem the ideals for the artist in culture that the elites of the prior century could show only by negation. Artists and their friends (hopefully including their friends in the churches) may now be uniquely positioned to break the malaise of the current polarization and develop a truly prophetic stance toward culture. It will require acting not just for shock and self-aggrandizement but for cultivation and common flourishing. Artists can become known instead as "citizen artists" who lead in society with their imagination and their work.[2]

Artists can admit to the failure of the culture wars stance and abandon it, instead creating opportunities for genesis moments in culture—moments in which dialogue can happen, caricatures can be discarded, and deeper concerns can be addressed. Artists can take the lead in showing generosity in such dialogues, offering opportunities and creating microcosms of true diversity. And finally, to be consistent with the three Gs of culture care, artists can think generationally, providing for a stronger foundation for deeper reflections in culture.

ᴑ ᴑ ᴑ

T. S. Eliot writes helpfully of just such a deeper view—of a common life and the common good—in *Notes Towards the Definition of Culture*: "If we take culture seriously, we see that a people does not need merely enough to eat . . . but a proper and particular *cuisine*. . . . Culture may even be described simply as that which makes life worth living."[3]

Today, what makes life worth living for artists is a dying ember. And bullet holes in our schools and high rates of suicide for sensitive populations such as teenagers remind us that cultural failure is no abstract issue. Casualties are mounting—Amy Winehouse, Philip Seymour Hoffman, and Robin Williams, to name a few from a sadly long list.

Only a few years ago I asked, What happened to the young woman with the operatic voice, a vibrant part of her church community, who stepped confidently onto the stage at the 1986 Grammy Awards? When we see Whitney Houston's life, her struggles, and her death played out in front of us, we shudder and lament. But how much of her journey is predicated on our own consumption of culture, a culture littered with the discarded bodies of gifted individuals? Now Whitney Houston's shocking death just before the 2012 Grammy Awards is only an afterthought in a growing list of celebrity artists prematurely lost to us.

We have done little to cultivate the soil of culture for the next generation, so efforts we make now to plant seeds of culture will likely not yield significant results for some time. This is a bleak assessment, but it may be encouraging to reflect on parallels in the natural world: for example, volcanic soil is highly fertile, and forest fires can benefit the ecosystem. The right conditions and care make rapid regeneration possible in the aftermath of many disasters.

Generative activity is transformative. But living into the ideal of a common life will demand much from each artist—and much from each of us in other spheres of influence. Destruction and dissolution are far easier than creation and connection. We need vision, courage, and perseverance. This is why the care and cultivation of culture begins with the care and cultivation of the soul.

5

SOUL CARE

We have just noted how artists have in recent years been pushed to the margins, where many have resorted to various efforts to shock or transgress to get attention. I have often noticed that when these same artists are placed in an environment of nurture, such as an arts residency, what they create has a different tone. These thoughts came together recently while I was considering culture care values, and I realized that much of what I speak about here flows out of conversations with my wife. Culture care principles are based in part on the therapeutic language I have heard my wife use in describing her work. That language of *care* is an extension of her bringing home that bouquet of flowers to care for our souls.

As a psychotherapist, Judy does not expect her clients to come in happy and smiling. Her clients come because they need help. At some level they are aware of the fragmentation that is disrupting their lives. My wife assumes that her clients will arrive upset, angry, and dysfunctional. She sees it as her work to help heal the wounds—and to do so she listens carefully and gives the clients their own work to do under her guidance.

Similarly, if our prevailing culture is wounded and dysfunctional, should we not expect that most cultural artifacts will speak of the ills of the world? Cultural catalyst Erwin McManus tells the story of a conversation he had with a young artist who was struggling to avoid making art to be used for propaganda. He wanted to create works that expressed authentic emotions. But the only emotions this artist thought of as authentic were negative: "anger, betrayal, fear." He had never thought to ask whether love or happiness could be true human experiences that could be portrayed with authenticity. And he was unable to connect with what makes life worth living (both figuratively and, sadly, literally).[1]

When we hear primarily of alienation and suffering, the temptation to despair is strong. But if we can listen carefully while holding on to hope, honest assessments of our cultural problems can point us to discoveries of self-awareness—including the recognition of innate longings that we have been attempting to satisfy in unhealthy ways—that can in turn lead to healing.

There are thus significant overlaps for culture care not only with creation care but with soul care, which is the spiritual development and psychological integration that can result when we diligently follow good guidance. The work of soul care, the work of both therapist and client, is extemporaneous. It cannot be linear but is rather an interactive and creative process that responds on an ongoing basis to the shifting needs of the soul. All effective care providers are in this sense artists of the soul.

One way to envisage culture care at work is to transpose our knowledge of mental health and spiritual formation to culture. Most people cannot escape dysfunction on their own, and untended emotional wounds are more likely to fester than to heal. On one hand, it is the job of the psychotherapist to map a path toward healing for the client, not to leave a hurting person fragmented, stuck along the journey, or trapped in perpetual dependency on therapy. But at the same time, psychological and emotional health—like spiritual growth—cannot be imposed from the outside. This is also true for culture.

One of the ways people who have experienced traumatizing events begin to find healing from symptoms like flashbacks and nightmares is by learning to retell the story of their traumatic encounters in a safe environment. This helps them move from involuntarily reexperiencing the emotional pain of the event to connecting the memory with supportive listeners and a larger framework of meaning. It helps them see the trauma as one episode in their larger life story rather than as defining their identity.

Similarly, culture care starts with the identification and articulation of brokenness. It creates a safe space for truth telling. But it does not stop there. It starts with listening and then invites people onward toward beauty, wholeness, and healing. As we become able to acknowledge the truth of our situation and can tell that story, we are encouraged to move into caring for artists and all other participants in the culture, into creating contexts for deeper conversation, into fostering spiritual growth, and sometimes into problem solving.

❧ ❧ ❧

A key reason that I connect culture care with Judy's work in soul care is that our experience of beauty depends on more than intellectual and technical accomplishments.

On an aesthetic level, learning to perceive deeper depths of beauty includes training or apprenticeship in the craft and tradition in which we are participating. A viewer may need to be shown how to open up himself or herself to certain forms of beauty, or to be trained in how to read a painting. A listener may need instruction in hearing tone and color in a symphony. A student may need to be trained to approach an object from different perspectives. A child or novice may need to be exposed to many instances of what others have recognized as beautiful before being able to form a coherent judgment. And of course anyone working in the arts will have to practice diligently.

But beyond this, our very state of being affects our ability both to perceive and to create beauty. If we doubt that beauty exists, for example, we will have a truncated experience even when we encounter it. And as I found in New York, it is possible to reach the point of rejecting beauty as ephemeral, saccharine, or naive and viewing its pursuit as archaic, unfashionable, or déclassé.

Appreciation of the depths of beauty is a condition of our physical, mental, and spiritual health—and of our physical, mental, emotional, relational, and spiritual maturity. We all begin immature and unformed. We all bear some degree of disorder. And we all bear a degree of responsibility to address this disorder. There is a saying that you cannot share what you do not have. Similarly, our maturity level sets a limit on the quality and expressiveness of the work we can produce.

We often think of great artists, musicians, and writers—those who have demonstrated the ability to express beauty—as great souls. Most or all of them faced, and many overcame, great disorder; we will encounter a few of their stories in the coming chapters. Wesley Hill, a professor at Trinity School for Ministry, recently told a story (it may be a legend) about a Yale student working under the great Old Testament scholar Brevard Childs. The student was unhappy with his grade and asked how he could improve his next essay. Childs replied, "Become a deeper person."[2]

How can we do this? Certainly not in isolation. In psychological terms, we need to do the work, to follow the path toward healing that is mapped out for us. This might include finding healthy people to emulate or safe spaces in which to incubate new expressions of creativity. It may involve imaginative exercises to extend empathy and combat narcissism. In spiritual terms, we need to respond in faith and take hold of the grace we are so freely given. This might include taking advantage of spiritual directors—personal trainers for the soul—or embracing some regimen of spiritual exercises and practical disciplines to build spiritual and moral muscles and bring order to our souls.

Soul care will require nurturing spaces for such formation—but I see these looking less like celebrity rehab clinics and more like working neighborhood gyms or Olympic training centers. Such spaces would feature purposeful, visionary leadership by active mentors and trainers committed to culture care. In each space, a community of peers would gather to work together and challenge each other to excellence and growth to prepare themselves for competition and collaboration.

A healthy and thriving culture is impossible without the participation of artists and other leaders who are educated intellectually, trained experientially, formed spiritually, and growing morally. Beauty is both a goal and a catalyst for each of these elements.

6

BEAUTY AS FOOD
FOR THE SOUL

*O*nce we see the connection of culture care with soul care, the next set of questions to ask becomes clear: What are we inviting people into? What sort of food does the soul need? What is beauty, and how does it feed that part of us that is more than instinct and appetite? How might beauty address personal and cultural fragmentation and dysfunction?

These questions have captivated people throughout recorded history, and those trying to tease out answers usually find themselves in deep and sometimes murky waters. Beauty is notoriously hard to pin down, and it is often spoken of together with other ultimate concerns, particularly the true and the good. Dallas Willard has even defined beauty as "goodness made manifest to the senses."[1]

How deeply intertwined these three core qualities are is debated, but experience shows that a lack of either truth or goodness (whether in quality of workmanship or in the moral sense) detracts from the beauty of a given artifact. Similarly, a lack of attention to beauty in presenting a truth hampers its appeal and adoption. And we have just discussed ways that a culture that downplays the pursuit of beauty also loses its appetite for truth and goodness.

If beauty is food for the soul, we can also think in terms of the many things we are still learning about the interaction between food choices and the health of body, mind, and spirit. When we are busy or distracted, it is easy to fall back on eating overly processed "convenience" foods. Their empty calories do little to strengthen our bodies and may indeed create unhealthy appetites or increase our vulnerability to clinical depression. Similarly, when feeding our souls we dare not substitute surface attraction—that which is effortlessly appreciated and soon exhausted of virtue—for true beauty. Instead we need to cultivate an appetite for the best soul food, whole and unprocessed, requiring time to absorb and digest.

Much more can and should be said on this theme, but for now it will be helpful instead to draw together the threads implicit in our discussion so far and offer a working definition of beauty to ground our work in culture care.

Beauty is the quality connected with those things that are in themselves *appealing* and desirable. Beautiful things are a *delight* to the senses, a *pleasure* to the mind, and a *refreshment* for the spirit. Beauty *invites* us in, capturing our attention and making us want to linger. Beautiful things are *worth* our scrutiny, rewarding to contemplate, deserving of pursuit. They inspire—or even demand—a response, whether sharing them in community or acting to extend their beauty into other spheres.

Beauty may not be embodied in an enduring form—a given bouquet of flowers will soon wilt, though a painting or poem can last for generations—but it is something we want to remember and something we would not want to change. Beauty is thus connected with *satisfaction*—which may point to the way beauty feeds the soul.

Beauty touches on some combination of qualities, difficult to quantify, of pattern, design, form, shape, color, sound, light, integrity, and relationship. It appeals to us at multiple levels, speaking to our intellect and our logical capacities as well as our emotions and spirit. While it is commonly connected more with our physical senses and the material world than with the world of ideas, people often appeal to beauty when talking about the pursuit of knowledge, and the best scientific and mathematical theories are called beautiful in their simplicity or elegance.

So far this definition is not controversial and could be embraced by people across a wide spectrum of belief. Let me next sketch out four important themes related to beauty and culture care. These are gratuity, stewardship, justice, and our response.

❧ ❧ ❧

A Christian understanding of beauty begins with the recognition that God does not *need* us, or the creation. Beauty is a gratuitous gift of the creator God; it finds its source and its purpose in God's character. God, out of his gratuitous love, created a world he did not need because he is an artist.

Beauty itself is not, in this sense, necessary. Sometimes it seems as if many people in the modern age have attempted to prove this point negatively—like modernist architects and city planners doing their best to demonstrate that any object that could be made beautifully could also be made without beauty.

But even if we would agree that beauty is not necessary to our daily survival, it is still necessary for our flourishing. Our sense of beauty and our creativity are central to what it means to be made in the image of a creative God. The satisfaction in beauty we feel is connected deeply with our reflection of God's character to create and value gratuity. It is part of our human nature. This is why our soul hungers for beauty.

Because it is gratuitous, beauty points beyond itself, beyond survival to satisfaction. We think of it in opposition to narrowness, scarcity, drudgery, and constraint. We think instead of what is expansive, generous, abundant, connected, and expressive. Beauty also connects us with the *why* of living. It points to discoveries waiting to be made about the creation. It points toward questions of right relationships, of ultimate meaning, and even of eternity. It points backward and outward and forward to our ultimate Source and Sustainer.

When we encounter beauty, we want to slow down and partake of its refreshment, to let it reorient us to our deepest longings and reconnect us to our deepest selves. And however undeveloped or distorted it is, our innate sense of beauty is what makes us struggle in the face of the utilitarian pressures of modernism, even when we cannot express ourselves and our longings in words.

In its gratuity and generosity, beauty—paradoxically—helps set boundaries on how we live. Our actions can be assessed based on whether or not they lead toward beauty. We can be challenged by comparisons of our work with works that reveal a higher standard. This may explain why many modernists overtly resist the very concept of beauty.

In pushing back against modernism, it may also be helpful to introduce an idea from the philosopher Roger Scruton. He defines beauty in part as that which repays contemplation for its own sake, and he claims that beauty and utility conflict only in the short run. Beauty may not be "practical," but he has noted that when people neglect beauty, they produce, ultimately, useless things. Focusing on mere function actually will consign an object to oblivion. Beauty, Scruton says, is what makes things last.[2]

～ ～ ～

I said earlier that beauty is a gift that we discover, receive, and *steward*. This is a claim that beauty is found both in nature and in culture. It is something that is given to us, and it is also something we human beings can add to—something we can cultivate.

God asks us to continue as he began. We have the ability and responsibility to create more (gratuitous) beauty. J. R. R. Tolkien, author of *The Lord of the Rings*, used the helpful concept of sub-creation.[3] In anything we make, we bring our creative energies, but we are always acting in stewardship of something that we have been given. At our best we work *with* our raw materials, honoring their properties and respecting their limits, not working against the grain or twisting them out of context. In short, we need to love both nature and culture to exercise a proper stewardship.

Recent thinking in agriculture offers some ideas that may transfer to the stewardship of culture. Localism acknowledges the unique character of each region and suggests that it is good to grow produce that is native to the place and in tune with the climate, natural soil, and local botany. Hothouse flowers or imported vegetables may be desirable when our local climate is inhospitable or some disaster has damaged local crops, but there is a virtue in local produce. It often tastes better. Eating locally seasonal foods seems to be better for our bodies.

Effective stewardship leads to generative work and a generative culture. We turn wheat into bread—and bread into community. We turn grapes into wine—and wine into occasions for joyful camaraderie, conviviality, conversation, and creativity. We turn minerals into paints—and paints into works that lift the heart or stir the spirit. We turn ideas and experiences into imaginative worlds for sheer enjoyment and to expand the scope of our empathy.

As in creation care, cultural stewardship includes trying to find our place in the wider ecosystem. It asks us to consider what we have been given and where we are situated. It will take human nature into account—acknowledging our true longings and limitations.

Another contemporary philosopher, Elaine Scarry, is known for connecting beauty with justice. Dr. Scarry spoke at the spring 2002 IAM conference at New York University, cosponsored by *Image Journal* and titled, audaciously at the time, "The Return of Beauty." (After September 11, beauty was much needed, and the contemporary art world seemed to rediscover it as a value.) One point of connection between beauty and justice, Scarry says, is that "beauty, sooner or later, brings us into contact with our own capacity for making errors."[4]

I resonate with this observation. An encounter with beauty can open the door of perception so that we are moved to turn from our errors and begin a journey toward the authentic. What Christians call "repentance"—from the Greek *metanoia*, to turn back—is often sparked by an encounter with the beautiful.

Ultimately, the reality of beauty prompted my own journey to faith. The link between beauty, justice, and our necessary response is a key value of culture care, but it was only while writing this book that I have become able to recognize and start to articulate it. A single gesture of generosity, the reminder of beauty in my life by Judy, opened a journey of exploration that led to my falling into faith in Christ.

My own failure to value beauty and to acknowledge it as a need for my life and my art led to many more struggles. I speak of this in several other writings, but the more I experienced beauty, especially the beauty that was being created through my own hands, the more alienated I felt from it. I did not have a model or category in which to receive beauty. It was only through my encounter of seeing Christ and his sacrifice in love for me—through my reading of *Jerusalem*, William Blake's last epic poem (1804)—that I saw the *beauty of sacrifice* in Christ.

I said earlier that Jesus is the source of beauty. As that source, Jesus is appealing, and knowing him brings delight—an assertion with consequences for the activities and approaches of every individual and community that reflects Jesus, not least the church.

My encounter with Christ's beauty, reflected in the Isaiah 61 passages I quoted earlier, has resulted in a series of shifts in how I view myself and the role of art in society. What I write here is the direct result of my own *metanoia*, a journey that was nourished by Judy's act of generosity.

෨ ෨ ෨

It will be helpful at this point to consider the goals that I have come to recognize in the years since I received that bouquet. What is it to which we should aspire as artists and creative catalysts (those who may not consider themselves artists but are still key cultural players)?

We can turn again here to Isaiah 61. In the same verse that talks about a crown of beauty, the prophet makes an explicit connection between beauty, suffering, and justice that speaks directly to a role the arts should be playing. Those who receive crowns of beauty are those who have been poor, brokenhearted, captive, mourning, grieving, and despairing—and the result of God's intervention is that these same people are to "be called oaks of righteousness." Part of the good news they hear is a work order. The purpose of the prophet's message—which Jesus says he fulfills—is a call to act for justice and renewal. Those who have suffered are the very ones who

> will rebuild the ancient ruins
>   and restore the places long devastated;
> they will renew the ruined cities
>   that have been devastated for generations. (Isaiah 61:3-4)

Even those who are still considering Jesus' claims will find a grounding for justice work in the cultivation of beauty. An encounter with beauty can show us what could be, and can make us rightly dissatisfied with the way things are. In the face of the undeniable and often unbearable human suffering all around us, we must still affirm beauty and work to make our culture reflect it. This is why a culture care approach will encourage truth telling about alienation, suffering, and oppression alongside truth telling about justice, hope, and restoration.

Certainly, some or all of our work should aim to surprise our jaded culture with delight and remind others of what we humans truly long for. Artists in the last century have been functioning in society to reveal brokenness; in this century, can they lead the way toward reconnection, reconciliation, and reintegration?

ဢ ဢ ဢ

In addition to gratuity, stewardship, and justice, a framework for beauty should also include the notion of sacrifice. Beauty, as poets in Japan saw a long time ago, is connected with death. The Japanese ideogram for beauty (美) is made up of two ideograms, the one for sheep (羊) laid on top of the one for large (大). Apparently, in China, where the ideograms originated, what was beautiful was a "fat sheep." In a culture in which eating meat was a rare occurrence, a fat sheep was supreme delight. But in Japan a deeper connection was made to the sacrifice of the sheep. I write about the details of Japanese refining of the ideogram in my book *Silence and Beauty*; in Japan, beauty is culturally connected with dying and sacrifice.

Sacrifices are needed to provide beauty in the world. In the following chapters, we will look at some roles through which these sacrifices might take place, roles that depend on the care and feeding of the soul. We will look at a new model for leadership as border care—building bridges and serving as messengers or ambassadors to separated groups, trying to find a way to the common good. We will look at language care—finding trade languages and a generative grammar to defuse the culture wars. And we will look at various means of stewardship of the wider ecosystem of our culture, including the cultivation of artists and business leaders who can be the custodians of culture.

7

LEADERSHIP FROM
THE MARGINS

*E*arlier I noted that artists have been pushed to the margins. Recently I was speaking with my colleague and collaborator Bruce Herman. He introduced me to an Old English word used in *Beowulf*: *mearcstapas*, translated "border-walkers" or "border-stalkers."[1] In the tribal realities of earlier times, these were individuals who lived on the edges of their groups, going in and out of them, sometimes bringing back news to the tribe.

Artists are instinctively uncomfortable in homogeneous groups, and in "border-stalking" we have a role that both addresses the reality of fragmentation and offers a fitting means to help people from all our many and divided cultural tribes learn to appreciate the margins, lower barriers to understanding and communication, and start to defuse the culture wars. Artists on the margins of various groups can be deputized (not conscripted) to represent tribal identities while still being messengers of hope and reconciliation to a divided culture.

Part of this role can be thought of in the terms of soul care. A psychotherapist, as an artist of the soul, needs to know the "tribal" reality that her clients are facing. In some sense, a broken marriage is due to the unresolved tension between two tribal identities. All marriages are crosscultural, so a good therapist will help raise to the surface the issues and resources of each culture in the relationship and then help the two conflicting cultures come together as complements. Marriage counseling happens in a generally trusting context where the husband and wife are both responding to the guidance of the therapist. But at a community level, and particularly when the tribes in conflict have not asked for a guide, a would-be societal therapist faces a deeply challenging task.

Mearcstapa is not a comfortable role. Life on the borders of a group—and in the space between groups—is prone to dangers literal and figurative, with people both at home and among the "other" likely to misunderstand or mistrust the motivations, piety, and loyalty of the border-stalker. But *mearcstapa* can be a role of cultural leadership in a new mode, serving functions including empathy, memory, warning, guidance, mediation, and reconciliation. Those who journey to the borders of their group and beyond will encounter new vistas and knowledge that can enrich the group.

In *The Lord of the Rings*, J. R. R. Tolkien introduces the shadowy figure of Strider the Ranger at an inn in the homely village of Bree, where the comfortable and hospitable innkeeper warns the travelers not to trust him. Strider is a *mearcstapa*, and it is in large part his ability to move in and out of tribes and boundaries that makes him an indispensable guide and protector and that helps him become an effective leader, fulfilling his destiny as Aragorn, high king of Gondor and Arnor, uniting two kingdoms. He even marries across tribes with his union to Arwen, daughter of Elrond Half-Elven.

Often artists are branded as "difficult people" in society, hard to pin down and notorious for being independent. In Tolkien's story, the travelers accept Strider as a guide only when they receive a letter that vouches for him. But Strider might speak for many artists in his comment to his reluctant new friends: "'But I must admit,' he added with a queer laugh, 'that I hoped you would take to me for my own sake. A hunted man sometimes wearies of distrust and longs for friendship.'"[2]

I am giving the name *mearcstapa* to a role that many artists and others have come to naturally. Many more who might thrive in this role go through life with their potential untapped or misused. But the leadership quality that lurks within them is too valuable to be dismissed or left dormant. Identifying and befriending those with this gifting, many of whom may start out awkward or ill-fitting, is critical to culture care. But to come to full maturity, a *mearcstapa* will need not only friendship but deliberate cultivation in community. Tolkien understood this; he tells us later in the story that Strider is supported in his role by other Rangers and had lived for many years training with the elves of Rivendell and Lórien. We have many "Striders" in our midst, and many in our communities and churches are suspicious toward them. We need to start seeing them as "Aragorns," potential great leaders.

Artists who come to embrace the role of *mearcstapa* and find support and training to walk it out can become leaders who make possible the reunification of divided kingdoms; they can be reconcilers of division and fragmentation. They can release great generativity and flourishing.

᠑ ᠑ ᠑

In the story of the good Samaritan that Jesus tells in Luke 10, we see a man who is considered by the listeners as "other" and "enemy" giving generous help to an injured man when religious professionals and the respected members of his own tribe fail him. Artists have a great capacity to see someone who is "other" as their neighbor in the sense that Jesus defines this role in the parable. They can follow his instruction to "do likewise" in showing mercy and making full recovery possible (Luke 10:37).

Where does this openness to the other come from in artists? Some may grow out of empathy earned because artists are themselves often exiled from a normative tribal identity. There is also training to extend that empathy. In art we constantly train ourselves to inhabit or portray the other. Artists learn to be adaptable and blend into an environment while not belonging to it, which also requires learning to speak new tribal languages.

This is an area with real dangers and real opportunities. Sometimes artists lose their connection with their original tribe and their core identity in adapting to a new environment. (I mentioned earlier Whitney Houston's struggles with success. Her case is all too common—though her legacy also includes many generative elements.) But if adaptability can be exercised without sacrificing one's core beliefs and ideological convictions, the experience will actually deepen such convictions. It will also mark a path toward a more perceptive and wider-scale view of culture.

The generosity of an artist in this sense can mean mediation in the culture wars, beginning by overcoming caricatures and injecting diversity, nuance, and even paradox into the nature of the conversation, and then moving on to teach society a language of empathy and reconciliation. Grounded artists can provide rallying points around which reconciliation can begin. Through such practices, they can become good Samaritans to a divided culture. Let's explore some fictional and biographical cases.

8

"TELL 'EM ABOUT THE DREAM!"

*Y*ou never really understand a person," Atticus Finch tells us in *To Kill a Mockingbird*, "until you consider things from his point of view . . . until you climb into his skin and walk around in it."[1]

In the book we see Atticus's daughter, Scout, running through the streets of Maycomb, Alabama, chasing her brother, Jem, and her friend Dill. "Maycomb County had recently been told that it had nothing to fear but fear itself," recalls Scout. There is an eye-of-the-storm stillness in the streets; slow, ambling folks who "shuffled in and out of the stores" and "took their time about everything. A day was twenty-four hours long but seemed longer."[2] The Great Depression has gripped the county, and it has been deeply wounded by World War I. There will be more conflicts to come.

Harper Lee's classic work brings the reader into the heart of that American struggle via an inquisitive, feisty, creative girl. Scout is a *mearcstapa* in the story, learning to lurk in and out of tribal identities divided by race. And Lee was herself working as a *mearcstapa* by writing to evoke empathy for all sides of the divide. *To Kill a Mockingbird* was published in 1960. Harper Lee remembered her country lawyer father, and in the character of Atticus Finch she translated the principles of justice and equality he taught her into great art. Lee set out to tell what she called a "simple love story," but the result was a powerful catalyst to transform a cultural mindset from bigotry to respect for human dignity.

Lee's art reshaped the world. Former Supreme Court justice Sandra Day O'Connor, for example, has said the book made her want to become a lawyer. The book also foreshadows Martin Luther King, Jr.'s "I Have a Dream" speech—anticipating it by three years. I see *To Kill a Mockingbird* as one of the twentieth century's great cultural artifacts for wrestling with issues of humanity and as a model to teach us how to speak with empathic creativity and transform the cultural river.

In the book Atticus Finch defends Tom Robinson, a man falsely accused of rape. Knowing that the town is conspiring to lynch him, Atticus "sits guard" in front of the jailhouse where Mr. Robinson is being held. He sets up a chair and reading light outside the cell window, creating a borderline. He is using a theatrical prop to make his case, if you will—bringing his living room right into the heart of the conflict. Creating this borderline and acknowledging the division is essential for reconciliation.

A mob gathers. Scout, Jem, and Dill walk right into that circle, making Atticus quite nervous. Scout then recognizes a face in the crowd: "Don't you remember me, Mr. Cunningham? I'm Jean Louise Finch. You brought us some hickory nuts one time, remember? . . . I go to school with Walter . . . he is your boy, ain't he? Ain't he, Sir?"[3]

Scout remembers that "Atticus had said it was the polite thing to talk to people about what they were interested in, not about what you were interested in."[4] Atticus had taught her empathy. So she speaks to Mr. Cunningham using a big word Atticus taught her: "entailment." Mr. Cunningham had brought the hickory nuts to Atticus in thanks for work Atticus had performed for the Cunningham family. Now Scout reminds Mr. Cunningham about entailment, or a swap of one work for another. It becomes a code to unlock his humanity, to help him remember. Scout also uses it to tap into his conscience, his awareness of how human beings should treat each other, with dignity and respect. And she defuses the situation in her determined innocence. Both Atticus and Scout bring a sense of humanity into the divide, and both are willing to be border-stalkers, communicating intentionally across boundaries.

ᔕ ᔕ ᔕ

Our culture has made progress of a sort since Harper Lee first wrote. Just as our views on pollution have changed, now a racial lynch mob is practically unthinkable. But some things do not change. Every age seems to find its own "other." The temptation to dispense a rough "justice" against some individual or group flares up whenever we lose our focus on our common humanity and succumb to fear.

Just like the mob in front of Tom Robinson's jail cell, our culture is still prone to create scapegoats, dodging our own culpability and responsibility for cultural or systemic problems by blaming them on innocent individuals or groups. We still blind ourselves to the dehumanizing forces this unleashes. With any given provocation, we are egged on by our instant, omnipresent media to unleash our basest instincts—we might think of them as cultural fight-flight-freeze responses—rather than committing ourselves to the slower process of seeking truth.[5] (One genuinely new thing is the virtual mob, which can be just as inhumane and culturally damaging as any physical mob.)

This self-debasement of our humanity in desperate and irrational fear of the other is a result of poor cultural stewardship. Little wonder that our culture is still bedeviled by cynicism, apathy, and anger. Cycles of violence and revenge are an ongoing reality. And when we focus on headlines and newsfeeds, we come to expect more of the same.

How would—how do—we respond when faced with an angry mob ready to commit an atrocity against us or some "other"? Would we want to fight back, fire against fire, hatred against hatred? Scout offers a better model. She does not even confront bigotry by arguing for justice. What she does in her naiveté is to step into the mob and remind people that they are her neighbors. She becomes a bouquet of flowers in the heart of conflict.

Reminding people of our common life—that we are neighbors first—is a task of culture care. We acknowledge openly the borders of our groups and acknowledge too the legitimate things that divide us. Our responsibility, then, is to rehumanize this divide. An emphasis on our role as *neighbor* as part of our identity begins this process by reminding us of our shared cultural and geographical spaces and the fact that proximity brings responsibility. Even apart from Jesus' call to love our neighbor, we know that our common flourishing depends on each other.

Scout defuses the situation by being fully human, fully a child. What she does naively, we must do courageously. Reconcilers of culture must speak like children—which is to say innocent of pretense and full of determined hope, confident in our own experience of beauty and joy in life, connected with the highest potential and calling of our common humanity, and expectant of finding this good in the lives of others.

Our arts and conversations should point toward beauty and healing. When they do, we may remind our neighbors, and ourselves, of who we are and who we can be when we exercise our capacity for empathy, gratitude, and generosity. This language of empathy is truly generative, and it is just as surprising in a cynical culture as is Scout's presence to the mob in the story. When such an unexpected voice breaks in, it can defuse culture-war language and emotions, rehumanize a mob, and provide a generative path for the collective energy. Such a voice can call our tribes closer to an attitude of cultural stewardship.

ॐ ॐ ॐ

The arts present the most powerful form of nonviolent resistance. Scout's actions in Harper Lee's creative lens—her willingness to step into a conflict and take a personal risk in order to call out *for both sides* their deepest humanity, highest ideals, and deepest longings—anticipated thousands of peaceful marches to come.[6]

Culture care affirms this language of empathy, which is a fruit of love toward the other. We need to create cultural contexts where this love toward those outside our tribe's borders is cultivated and modeled organically. A culture care environment will nourish and steward our abilities to dream even in the face of injustice, intolerance, and persecution.

Jesus told his followers, "I am sending you out like sheep among wolves. Therefore be as shrewd as snakes and as innocent as doves" (Matthew 10:16). Poets, artists, and creative catalysts can, like Scout, remain determinedly innocent as doves while being wise as serpents in using their creativity. Reminders of beauty can present justice in words, images, and songs that draw us in and captivate our attention until their truth can reach our hearts and transform our communities. Culture care is the logical extension of nonviolent resistance to injustice.

ॐ ॐ ॐ

In August 1963, prior to giving his "I Have a Dream" speech at the march on Washington, the Rev. Dr. Martin Luther King Jr. found himself exhausted by a series of setbacks, imprisonments, oppressions, and disappointments. He was so physically worn out that he spent many hours simply resting while his followers wrote the speech he was to give to the historic gathering. One of his close aides, Clarence Benjamin Jones, said that "the logistical preparations for the March were so burdensome that the speech was not a priority for us," and "on the evening of Tuesday, August 27 [twelve hours before the march], Martin still didn't know what he was going to say."[7] After walking a few miles to the Lincoln Memorial, he stood to read the prepared text, but he knew something was not right.

Mahalia Jackson, the great gospel singer who sang before he spoke, stood behind Dr. King throughout the speech. As he read, she kept on yelling, "Tell 'em about the dream, Martin; tell 'em about the dream!" At the end of the prepared speech, Dr. King put down his text and began to speak extemporaneously; the energy of the listening crowd empowered him, and the result was the "I Have a Dream" we know today.

Imagine that—an artist pushing a tired preacher to preach from his heart. Dr. King was an artist of the dream, but it took another artist to recognize the artistry that was being held back by the context of the gathering.

Artists need to stand behind the podiums of preachers, teachers, and leaders and remind them to "tell 'em about the dream!" Part of our calling is to remind leaders of what they are marching toward to begin with, to reach into the deepest recesses of *their own* visions. Sometimes we may need to remind them to put down their prepared text. Artists who operate as *mearcstapas* can exhort in this way, in and out of a prepared tribal language into a visionary, extemporaneous jazz language of the heart. That music invites all to become extemporaneous artists of care.

ᔆ ᔆ ᔆ

One cold, rainy evening in New York City in 2010, I was invited
to serve on a panel for a special screening of *Countdown to Zero*, a
film about nuclear disarmament. The friend who organized the
meeting was disappointed by the attendance; only about thirty
people came. He apologized for the low turnout to the crowd and
to the panel, which also included civil rights leader Jesse Jackson.
Jackson stopped him. "I remember that day when Martin gave his
famous sermon at the Riverside Church," Jackson said. "There were
only about thirty people then too."

The panel went on to discuss an initiative by President Ronald
Reagan and President Mikhail Gorbachev to eliminate nuclear
weapons. At one point Jackson spoke up again. "It was only when
Marvin Gaye started to sing that song ["What's Going On"] that
our civil rights movement became a true movement." He looked me
straight in the eye and said, "We need artists because they give us
songs to sing to."

Connecting justice with beauty is essential. Any cause we believe in needs a song that everyone can sing, a song to march to or
rally around, a song that will draw people in so they can learn to
care. Artists are the ones to provide the music. But artists are not
present just to entertain the crowd; like Mahalia Jackson, they can
play a role of revealing the heart of a movement. This is possible
because they, as *mearcstapas*, must learn not only to speak tribal
languages but also to trade languages and songs that connect
people across boundaries. Artists are, in this sense, uniquely prepared to create beauty that is universal or points to the universal.
They write songs that everyone can sing.

ᔆ ᔆ ᔆ

Artists are themselves leaders: they may never inspire with a speech, preach from a pulpit, or own a company, but they are leaders by the sheer fact of their awareness and observation and because of the stories they tell and the language and symbols they create. Psychologist Howard Gardner, creator of the "multiple intelligences" theory, writes:

> Indeed, creators and leaders are remarkably similar. Both groups seek to influence the thoughts and behaviors of other people. Both are, accordingly, engaged in the enterprise of persuasion. Moreover, each leader or creator has a story to tell: A creator is contributing to the story of a chosen domain; a leader is creating a story about his group. Finally, embodiment is important for both groups: A leader must embody her stories in her daily life; a creator must embody his story by carrying out work in his domain. The difference lies in the directness of this influence.[8]

Mahalia Jackson's prompting of Dr. King released him to speak from the heart. But her own powerful artistic work, like Marvin Gaye's later, was even more so an "enterprise of persuasion," an effort, as she said, to "break down some of the hate and fear that divide" people.[9] It was the work of a border-stalker. She used her indirect influence as a creator to become a more direct leader. And she did so by staying true to her core convictions.

Not all artists can or should follow Jackson into overt leadership, but she is still someone all of us should emulate. Influence of any kind imposes responsibility, and Jackson is a model for influence that is well-invested. Artists have a responsibility to use their persuasive pull to create the "world that ought to be" and to avoid the misuse of their abilities, which can become so self-destructive. One sure way to do so is by using their influence to illuminate the path of empathy.

9

TWO LIVES AT THE MARGINS

*A*rtists as *mearcstapas* can provide significant cultural language or even new operative principles for our societies and churches. Harper Lee and Mahalia Jackson saw beyond their current realities. So too in their own times and places did the poet Emily Dickinson (1830–1886) and the painter Vincent van Gogh (1853–1890).

Emily and Vincent are concrete examples of *mearcstapas* living in times that prefigure ours. They anticipated the full flowering of modernity, intuiting the rise of utilitarian pragmatism and creating works that spoke—and are still speaking today—against dehumanization. Neither of them fit well with their culture. Both longed for their gifts to be acknowledged and cared for, but they left behind abundant evidence in their letters that this incompatibility arose from greater purposes, not always articulable, to which they felt called.

Both Emily and Vincent struggled in particular to fit into the context of their churches. I like to use their examples to point out some future possibilities of artists' roles in society and in the church. Their vision was creative and artistic, but it was also theological and intimately connected with what they considered to be true worship.

IN THE DASHES

I see in the works of Emily Dickinson and Vincent van Gogh a pilgrimage toward the margins of society, often intentionally moving away from their own secure borders of familial tribal culture. Vincent began to learn to draw when he, as an evangelist, spent time in the Belgian coal mines, sharing in the miserable darkness of the miners. Emily withdrew into a corner of her small room, yet in doing so she took flight in her poems.[1] Notice this 1879 poem on a hummingbird:

> A Route of Evanescence
> With a revolving Wheel—
> A Resonance of Emerald
> A Rush of Cochineal—
> And every Blossom on the Bush
> Adjusts its tumbled Head—
> The Mail from Tunis—probably,
> An easy Morning's Ride—[2]

This playful poem is an illumination. The mention of emerald and cochineal—burgundy dye extracted from a little Indian beetle, a dye that I use in my work—reinforces the pictorial quality of her poem. Her mention of Tunis, a North African city once known for piracy, connotes exotic adventure within a place where splendors of the past are hidden and revealed. Because Emily spent her life in Amherst, Massachusetts, Tunis serves more as a mental than physical location. Her references to foreign cities are comparable to van Gogh's perceptions of "Japan"—a foreign place of paradise inaccessible to the artist. The "route of evanescence" of a hummingbird lends such exotic splendor to a mail carrier's ordinary "morning ride."

This is a good example of how the very structure of her writing echoes what she observed in nature—the iambic rhythm of these verses, the slant rhymes (wheel/cochineal, head/ride) alternating between verses, and the alliterations (resonance/rush, tumbled/ Tunis) weaving in and out, just like a hummingbird seeking nectar.

An artist's *mearcstapa* journey may not be a physical one. In her poetry, by identifying herself with a hummingbird Emily is moving toward the margins. From her small window, she takes us on an imaginative border-stalking journey. The news of that far land ("mail from Tunis") is both enticing and ominous. The "revolving wheel" reminds us of Ezekiel's vision, and, as in all her poems, she draws from a language learned as a daughter of Amherst Calvinists.[3] Her rhythms are taken from hymns she learned to play on the piano. It is also evident that her poems are confessions of how she deemed herself unfit for the church and chose not to participate even as the Great Awakening expanded in the North, and of her deep mourning for the costly sacrifice of the Civil War.

§ § §

When I visited Emily Dickinson's Amherst home, our group was taken to her room on the second floor. There, along with a small bed, is a replica of her desk, the delicate, single-drawer wooden writing table she used to write her poems. It is made of cherry wood, seventeen and a half inches square.

One reminder from Emily's life is that one needs nothing more than a small and dedicated space to make a significant impact in culture. She had neither publisher nor an encouraging writing environment—no one even knew she was writing so much poetry. But she had her desk and a lamp by which to get up, every day at three in the morning, to write.

In order to be generative, we may have to find ways to protect our creativity in light of limited resources. When I speak to artists' groups, I often ask, "Do you have your own 'seventeen-and-a-half-inch' desk dedicated to your craft?"

❧ ❧ ❧

Emily's well-documented struggles with faith place her at the edge of the discourse between faith and culture; yet it is precisely because of her struggles that she is valuable to the church and to anyone who desires to wrestle deeply with faith, art, and culture.

I have found as a local leader in communities and churches that others do not know what to do with you if you identify yourself as an artist. Things go much more smoothly if you are a lawyer or accountant. In church and parachurch ministry leadership training, those who do not fit into the agenda of preset programs are often marked as hard to disciple, or even as unfaithful.

Emily Dickinson, as a young girl attending a prestigious school in Amherst, experienced something similar, though more pointed. Her schoolmaster, Mary Lyons, was the founder of Mount Holyoke Female Seminary—and an evangelist. Lyons created categories for young girls and regularly divided her students into three public groups: committed followers of Christ ("Christians"); those hoping to become Christians ("Hopers"); and those who were without hope of becoming Christians ("No-Hopers"). Lyons placed Emily in the third category.[4]

Emily refused to participate in the waves of revivalism that swept Amherst and in which family members and friends experienced conversion. She wrote to her friend Jane Humphrey, "Christ is calling everyone here, all my companions have answered, even my darling Vinnie believes she loves, and trusts him, and I am standing alone in rebellion."[5]

Maintaining her integrity alone surely took a measure of courage. That "rebellion" may have been awakened early by the sudden death of Emily's thirteen-year-old friend Sophia Holland, an event that affected her so deeply that she fell ill and had to take time off from school. She was then an exceptionally private but articulate girl, whose early childhood letters demonstrate her enthusiasm for learning and writing through witty and verbose run-on sentences.

Reading her life's letters is an ongoing encounter with death. One sees the run-on sentences replaced by multiple dashes. These dashes remained her unique expression and identity—she saw herself in the dashes, in the liminal, transitional space between life and death. In theory, each death could have been an opportunity to apply the Puritan teaching of seeking the eternal, but Emily felt each loss so keenly that instead she came to deeply question God's goodness and was drawn further into lament and isolation.

As she matured in her rejection of Calvinist theology, her satirical language sharpened. But her rebellion was as much against the rigid and imprecise categories by which people try to obscure the world's complexity and suffering. Such categories can become attempts to reduce the wheels of Ezekiel's vision, in all their beauty and terror, to the regulated gears of a grandfather clock. They are attempts to cage a hummingbird.

INTO THE STARRY NIGHT

Not much later but in another corner of the earth, Vincent van Gogh painted, haunted by the parallel specter of his own liminal existence. While Emily Dickinson chose to stay at home, Vincent journeyed far from his home in the Netherlands, first as an evangelist among the coal miners in Belgium and ultimately to Arles, France, where he met his early death.

Not many know that Vincent was born into a line of Dutch Reformed pastors and that he himself trained for the pastorate. It was only when the church elders rejected his call that he turned to work as an evangelist. He lived among the poor with Franciscan devotion. But the authorities who sent him were appalled by the squalid

conditions he chose to share. They rejected him again and pronounced him "unfit for the dignity of the priesthood."

The double rejection by the church of his desire to fully incarnate
himself in the lives of coal miners must have been deeply painful.
Little wonder that he, like Emily, came to reject "the God of the
clergymen."[6] But he did not lose his awareness of God's presence in
the lives of the poor, nor his sense of God urging him to love others.
It was while toiling in the Belgian coal mines that he began to draw
portraits of the miners. He was not at that point formally trained in
painting or drawing and yet, as he drew, he discovered that visually
he could communicate more deeply about the compassion he felt
for humanity than he could verbally in the pulpit. "I feel that there
is nothing more truly artistic than to love people," he wrote.[7]

Art became a way for Vincent to capture, even by candlelight, the
genesis moments hidden behind every darkened face—a way to tap
into the potential of each moment, to see afresh life's struggles in
the light of Christ's presence. His paintings are color-filled parables
of genesis moments, generatively given to us in flesh with canvas
and paint. By the time of his tragic death, he had devoted only three
years of his life to the paintings that he is known for, the works now
in the collections of museums all over the world.

ↄ ↄ ↄ

Time spent in consideration of Vincent's famous *Starry Night* can
become a journey into the heart of a *mearcstapa*. The painting is set
in Arles, France. Notice that at the very center of the painting is a
white Dutch Reformed church. Vincent imported a church building
from his childhood, pasting it into the French landscape to create a
parable of his own life.

If you obscure the church by placing a finger over it, the painting
falls apart visually. The church is the only vertical form, aside from

the dominant cypress tree on the left, which juts out to break the horizontal planes. The tree and the church are the two forms that connect heaven and earth. Without the church, the cypress takes over the swirl of movement and there is no visual center to hold the painting in tension.[8]

Notice too how the homes surrounding the church are lit with warm light. The church is the only building in the painting that is completely dark. Herein lies Vincent's message, particular to the reality of being a border-stalker: the Spirit has left the church—at least the building—but is active in nature. If you follow the visual flow of the painting, your eye will cycle upward, still anchored by the church building. Your gaze will come to rest in the upper right corner, on the Sun/Moon. This is not just a moon, nor a sun, but a combination. Vincent wanted to show that the Spirit of God transcends even nature—that in the resurrection, in the New Earth and the New Heaven, a complete new order will shape the things to come.

On June 23, 1888, Vincent wrote to Émile Bernard, a younger artist:

(But seeing that nothing opposes it—) supposing that there are also lines and forms as well as colors on the other innumerable planets and suns—it would remain praiseworthy of us to maintain a certain serenity with regard to the possibilities of painting under superior and changed conditions of existence, an existence changed by a phenomenon no queerer and no more surprising than the transformation of the caterpillar into a butterfly, or of the white grub into a cockchafer.[9]

You and I are caterpillars about to be transformed into butterflies. We are on the threshold of seeing what biblical scholar N. T. Wright calls the post-resurrection reality of "life *after* 'life after death.'"

Vincent painted this "superior and changed condition of existence" as already here—but not yet fully so. He developed a visual diction that serves as a bridge between our current condition and a future transformed, genesis condition. He envisioned the transformation and by faith painted the world to come, as a *mearcstapa* walking the borders between earth and heaven. He also depicted a world that he was intuiting, a world in which the church still holds things together structurally but in which the light has gone out of the church building.

10

OUR CALLING IN THE
STARRY NIGHT

*A*rt poses questions. It probes into our lives as living parables. One question we need to face is, *What do we do if Vincent is right?* What do we do in a culture in which the light of the Spirit has departed church buildings and gone swirling instead into nature, into life's margins? What do we do in a culture in which the church is viewed as only a lifeless structural memory of the moral underpinnings that keep the world from falling apart?

For we are living in the world Vincent depicted. The church has kept the structure of truth, but we have largely lost touch with the Spirit in creating beauty. The church is no longer where the masses come to know the Creator of beauty. Tim Keller, my former pastor, says that Christians have invited in Jesus as our Savior, but we also need to invite him in as our Creator.

Many have noted that members of our emerging generations are not eager to join a church. The fastest growing denomination, I am told, is "none." These younger people show little interest in denominationalism, and yet it does not seem that they are done with Jesus or the life of the Spirit. They have far more investment in seeking justice and caring for our environment than did my generation.

Perhaps many in the younger generations are becoming *mearcstapas*, artists of the borders and margins.

USEFUL OR VALUABLE?

In recent times, the arts have been seen as useful to the economy—but that surely misses the point of why we need to care for culture. Evaluating the arts based on an economic metric makes utility the bottom line, distorting our vision of the world that ought to be.

Utilitarian pragmatism is tied to a world in which vision is stripped of transcendence. Before the modern age in the West, the narrative of Christendom provided a vision of the world in which the "bottom line" was the full thriving of humanity. Lacking that vision, we have become accustomed to a reality where anything and anyone not valued at the moment can be disposable.

Sometimes we become aware of our own unconscious choice of utility and fragmentation over beauty and thriving by our reactions, just as my reaction to Judy's care revealed my assumptions. Often our initial intent is appropriate: pragmatic and responsible decision making. Feeding ourselves over the coming weekend is good. But that is not our "chief end" (in the famous words of the Westminster Shorter Catechism). Our calling, simply as humans—and more so as followers of Christ—is wider than our career and our survival, even in the modern age.

Utilitarian thinking is often disguised, but it still can result in lifelong entrapment if it is allowed in. Take the example of college. Most of us have been pragmatists, seeing college as a transactional entity in which the student spends four years of time and tuition to receive back a lucrative career. Parents advise their children to major in something "useful" rather than in the humanities, often under threat of withholding financial support. Desiring a sustainable career is noble, but such recommendations debase education—and our humanity. The pragmatic goal of having a useful degree can calcify into a dogma—or worse, reaffirm an unquestioned assumption—that you are only worthwhile if you are useful.

This is one of the effects of living in a culture where usefulness is the highest virtue. We are too prone to see a human being or human endeavor as worthwhile only as it is useful to the whole, whether that be a company, family, community, or even a church. The corollary is that individuals who do not meet this standard are "other," an attitude that results effectively in their exile from the functioning, "normal" world. Those who are disabled, those who are oppressed or weakened, or those who are without a voice are soon implicitly regarded as useless, and then as disposable.

Little wonder that some groups are pushing to grant our elderly and disabled people the "right to die," and that many are willing to be persuaded by arguments like those being made by philosopher Peter Singer and atheist evangelist Richard Dawkins for the elimination of children with Down syndrome. Suffice it to say that such arguments are logical only if we grant the dogma that we are trapped with limited resources in a materialist world where those who are considered useless take up resources needed for normal human beings. Too often, belief in such a world calls into being a utilitarian machinery of homogeneity, manipulation, and control run by those who presume to speak for the human species or the environment. But many of us, or perhaps all of us, will be deemed useless at some level in such a model.

CALLED BEYOND UTILITY

Culture care values reach far beyond materialism to the ultimate human value of love—toward a generative reality. Artists know instinctively that beauty, delight, and wonderment lie beyond the resources we assume we have, so they are often the whistleblowers who bring constricted and distorted visions to our attention. Their intuitions give birth to music, art, dance, and poetry that defiantly and joyfully reach beyond the closed boundaries of nature into the mystery of existence. Artistic expressions are signposts declaring what it is to be fully human.

Art is ultimately not "useful." It serves no practical function. This is why it is indispensable, especially in the modern age. Dana Gioia has rightly said that we "do not provide arts education to create more artists, though that is a byproduct. The real purpose of arts education is to create complete human beings capable of leading successful and productive lives in a free society."[1] We provide arts education so that we can have better teachers, doctors, engineers, mothers, and fathers. Arts are not a luxury but a path to educate the whole individual toward thriving. They are needed simply because a civilization cannot be a civilization without the arts. A great civilization is an art form of the highest order.

Business, education, and even the arts "industry" are driven (sometimes unawares) by utilitarian thinking. Even in defining *calling* today we often succumb to pragmatism. I have often heard church leaders say that if you do not have an opportunity to find an audience for your gifts, this is a sign that you are not called to that field of endeavor. Respond to the "needs" of the world, they advise. Had Emily and Vincent followed such pragmatic advice, we would not have their art today. Neither found an audience for their art in their lifetime, but they were indeed called to their art, and there is much to learn from their journeys—not least because of their unfulfilled promise.

Mearcstapas are *called* into the margins, into stalking the borders, moving between traditional tribes and the unknown. Vincent and Emily created in response to their own internal compasses, their own urgency of need to create. They both followed, quite consciously, the ultimate master *mearcstapa*, Jesus. They simply could not follow any other path.

Artists are often mislabeled as impractical because their intuition senses cultural realities before these are manifested in society. And certainly Emily and Vincent saw the true needs of their culture. They were guided by the Spirit, who spoke into their art and showed them the fractured tribal realities of our emerging modern time, to which they responded by speaking a prophetic language of reconciliation.

In their lifetimes Emily and Vincent were forced to operate in predetermined categories, strictly limited domains of how they were to serve God. Such categories, while often created with the best of intentions, are reductionist. They limit how we view humanity, not to mention God, and do not take into account the deep wrestling with faith, or its lack, that is so often part of the *mearcstapa* journey. Artists often confound pragmatic labels and bristle against the in-built dehumanization and fragmentation of categories. In that sense, all artists are *mearcstapas*, guiding us toward a world of abundance and complexity.

Younger artists often ask me whether their art is "good enough," and whether they are called to be an artist. My answer is, "If you are not sure, you are not called." That may seem harsh, but the reality of the arts requires that we follow our calling no matter what others think or even what we believe ourselves. When art is simply what we must do to stay true to ourselves, it is a calling.

It is not surprising that Emily and Vincent—and their art—were marginalized, for both intuited that such an exiled existence was the only way to remain consistent with their humanity given the cultural pressures of their time. Yet more than a century later these two exiled souls still speak eloquently to what our hearts long for. Emily's poems give us words to express our own resistance to utility. Vincent's paintings offer parables of beauty that sow seeds of authentic being into our wounded, dehumanized souls. Their works are antidotes to the utilitarian drive for commercial and ideological gain, remedies for the poison in the river of culture. They offer our dying culture unfading bouquets, gifts of enduring beauty that we do not want to refuse.

ᔥ ᔥ ᔥ

Every challenge is an opportunity to exercise generative thinking, to think through the fears and seek out the light that still shines, however obscured. The psalmist tells us that "the heavens declare the glory of God" (Psalm 19:1). If the church is darkened, perhaps we should focus on where the Spirit is moving and pay attention to where the colors are the most intense. The gospel reality speaks not just of what we do inside our churches but also of the presence of the divine already evident in nature and in all human creativity.

In a world in which churches are seen as darkened, we cannot practice "Sunday" faith and live as if Christ were not present in the rest of the week. We need to acknowledge the presence of grace in the darkest of areas, even—especially—in the areas we would rather hide from God. Instead of speaking of God primarily in personal life and church settings, we must proclaim God as the source of all illuminating life. We must find God in the very fabric of our callings as teachers, as nurses, as engineers, as artists, and as writers. We must see our occupations as part of the glorious reality in which God has already manifested the Spirit's incorruptible visage.

The church is not a building but the collective souls of the people whom God is calling to deep life and eternal fellowship with himself. Whether we are politicians, dancers, entrepreneurs, or plumbers, we are called into the starry night of our complex existence, as we too swirl into the darker mystery of our twenty-first-century vista. Because the "heavens declare the glory of God" we must be fragrant torches of truth and justice, carrying the aroma of beauty outside of the walls of our institutions. We can also bring our small offerings as lighted candles back to darkened church sanctuaries. The darker the building, the more pronounced such small acts of service will seem.

We can follow Christ's call, creating in love, as Vincent did— loving the world that rejected him and longing to be at home in the church, the only building without light. Christ, the Light of the world, is the ultimate *mearcstapa*, a shepherd-artist, border-stalking our tribal existence and bringing the light of the good news from the new tribe that is already here and yet to come. Christ's light will shine through every darkness and will not be extinguished.

の の の

Western Christianity in the twentieth century fell into an "adjective" existence, with Christian music, Christian art, Christian plumbers, and so on. Even today artists are often valued *in* the church only if they create art *for* the church, or at least "Christian art." We cannot "use" the arts for evangelism or discipleship any more than we can "use" a human being for utilitarian purposes. Culture care will mean moving away from such labels. There is no need to disown these terms absolutely, but we do need to realize that these categories in themselves are concessions to modernist pressures. They are a voluntary surrender to utilitarian pragmatism, and their use leads only to disdain and indifference. Ultimately, these terms undermine our mandate to infuse all of life with Christ's presence.

I am not a Christian artist. I am a Christian, yes, and an artist. I dare not treat the powerful presence of Christ in my life as an adjective. I want Christ to be my whole being. Vincent van Gogh was not a Christian artist either, but in Christ he painted the heavens declaring the glory of God. Emily Dickinson was not a Christian poet, and yet through her honest wrestling, given wings in words, her works—like Vincent's, like Harper Lee's, like Mahalia Jackson's—speak to all the world as integrated visions of beauty against injustice.

It is time for followers of Christ to let Christ be the noun in our lives, to let our whole being ooze out like a painter's colors with the splendor and the mystery of Christ, the inexhaustible beauty that draws people in. It is time to follow the Spirit into the margins and outside the doors of the church.

11

OPENING THE GATES

What kind of a framework is needed to guide *mearcstapas*—to prepare them for success on their mission?

Recently an artist friend noted that in John 10, the parable of the shepherd and his sheep, Jesus speaks of a reality in which the gate is opened into the world, and he states, "I am the gate for the sheep" (John 10:7). The open gate is why a sheep may leave the flock and be lost (as in Luke 15). The shepherd's job is to guide sheep through the gate and beyond, to help them find the best grass, and to protect them—not to keep them shut in their pen. The pen has a clear function, but we do not need a good shepherd if the sheep are always locked up to be safe from harm.

Jesus, however, promises safety both inside and outside the sheepfold: "I am the Gate. Anyone who goes through me will be cared for—will freely go in and out, and find pasture" (John 10:9 *The Message*). The word here translated "cared for" ("saved" in many translations) means to preserve something safe and unharmed, to keep something from being lost, and also to cure, heal, or restore to full health. The sheep in this image are made safe explicitly for the purpose of going out and coming in—to cross borders, we might say—so they can thrive.

In recent years, many churches and communities have missed this point. We have created rigid tribal boundaries with high barriers and closed gates to keep our sheep in the pen, safe from the wider world. Ironically, closed gates mandate the extra labor and expense of bringing in stale, dry fodder—everything "Christian" needed to feed the flock— for sheep who should be grazing green pastures for themselves.

This leaves our lively young sheep with a perceived choice between complying with a community's norms and starving culturally, and leaping the fence to get cultural nourishment. Our call as leaders and parents is instead to open the gate and guide them to the greater pastures.

Are we willing as a community or as churches to do that? Opening the gate will mean accepting a loss of control. It will mean exposing our children and our students to certain dangers. They will mix with other flocks, and sometimes we may have to go look for one that gets lost and "leave the ninety-nine" others behind (Luke 15:4). We will confront variable weather, predatory presences, and our own limits as shepherds. But the Good Shepherd promises to journey with us. Will we rely on him to do as he says?

It is not just the border-stalkers but all of us in the sheepfold who need to "go in and out" for our flourishing. If we can raise and train *mearcstapas* in their challenging role, this gifted group of folks may be able to learn to read the weather and inform us of dangers and opportunities, so that the whole flock will be better able to navigate the outer world of culture.

C.J.

Our second son, C.J., was just such a child.[1] I remember walking with him in the streets of New York City. Even as a young child he noticed things that I ignored, like homeless people or graffiti. He showed an early inclination to music and art, often bringing his skateboard to the edges of Manhattan and crossing into Brooklyn (well before Brooklyn was hip). He is a *mearcstapa*.

C.J. had, as he would readily admit, a very colorful teenage life. He struggled with his faith and his church commitments. During some dark days in his teens he violated many boundaries, and I feared at one point that I had lost him as a son. Those days were some of the most challenging of my life as a parent, but I also now recall them, as I write this, as some of the most rewarding. Even though C.J. has now "come home" in many ways, he still wrestles deeply with issues of faith and art. Today, a college graduate with degrees in music composition and philosophy, he is producing and writing his "collage" music in Seattle.

When he was about twelve, C.J. became interested in what would become hip-hop music. When he came to me with his interest, Judy and I decided to "train up a child in the way he should go" (Proverbs 22:6 ESV; meaning not "the way *we* think he should go"). I knew very little about that musical world, but we told him that he was welcome to listen to any song as long as he shared it with us and we could discuss it. (We did not give this permission to either his older brother or younger sister, although they too would grow into creative human beings. It was something only C.J. was allowed to do early.) I also arranged for a friend who was studying for a PhD in composition from Columbia University to come every Saturday and teach C.J. music theory.

I asked a pastor friend in the Newark slums if he could recommend any up-and-coming musicians. One he named was Kanye West, then an unknown from Chicago. I began to listen to West, then Eminem, Lauryn Hill, and Outkast. I never expected to be listening to explicit versions of many of their songs on my computer;

I often struggled with hip-hop and the lifestyle and language choices of which the art form spoke. C.J. warned me of these things even as a young person, noting too that "non-explicit" versions lack the power and eloquence of the originals. I have come to realize that he was right.

As a *mearcstapa* C.J. guided me into the world of hip-hop, and he continues to do so. When he went to college, he and his girlfriend realized that the university culture offered only two options: library culture, to get straight As, or frat culture, to drink and relieve stress. There was no alternative. So C.J. began to experiment with a Friday evening gathering called "Bankwet" (spelled differently each time), with hip-hop/rap performances, poetry readings, and art. He mentored many creative types, leading them to develop their craft. His girlfriend, a straight-A theater student, opted out of the stage production role she could have had in order to make her senior thesis a guerrilla theater project that exposed what university students were truly thinking and struggling with.

When Judy and I arrived for C.J.'s graduation, he and his friends spontaneously gathered all the folks involved in the Bankwet group. They performed for us, and together we celebrated their time at the university. What I noticed, to my delight, was that this group of creatives was the most diverse (culturally and racially) of any I have known at this university. C.J. and his friends instinctively brought together all the school's "tribes."

It would not be true to say that every decision our children have made aligns with my faith and values; but a reality of dealing with border-stalkers is that often they do not toe the line of conventionality. But as they hold to deeper values, they have the capacity to show us the possibilities, the green pastures, that exist beyond our tribal norms.

"I HAVE OTHER SHEEP"

The visible church is the sheepfold.[2] For too long we have held the gate shut and our members, especially children like C.J., have been starving culturally because we have lacked a proper guiding theology to explore and graze the cultural fields. We need to be reminded regularly that the Holy Spirit is active well beyond our walls and that God continually blesses all human beings, regardless of where they are in relationship with him.

Just as an ecosystem necessitates complexity and dependency of interaction, visible and invisible, so with the culture at large: God provides for us both inside and outside the visible church. In the lavishness—the gratuitousness—of God's common grace, the Holy Spirit is active in the wider culture as well, making green the grass outside the fold. Through the Holy Spirit's guidance and his filling of our lives with God's love, the Good Shepherd can lead us into the best pastures in the furthest reaches of culture.

In Matthew 5:45, Jesus tells us that God "causes his sun to rise on the evil and the good, and sends rain on the righteous and the unrighteous." This passage is often used by Christians to ground a theological understanding of common grace, but many discussions of this topic miss the connection with what Jesus says immediately before this: "You have heard that it was said, 'Love your neighbor and hate your enemy.' But I tell you, love your enemies and pray for those who persecute you, that you may be children of your Father in heaven" (Matthew 5:43-45).

If we are to follow Jesus, we must practice living in the light of common grace, and we must therefore learn practically how to love our enemies. This love begins in recognition that our enemies have the ability to become a part of God's church, his flock, as God's Spirit reconciles them to himself. Even those who are currently

God's enemies are people we need to treat as creatures God made and loves. These enemies, these "others," are among Jesus' "other sheep," those "not of this sheep pen," the sheep he promises to bring in (John 10:16).

The Holy Spirit is active at the margins of our churches, drawing people in. When we hold our gate shut, we not only starve our own sheep but our pursuit of safety becomes a barrier to entry for Jesus' other sheep.

ᔮ ᔮ ᔮ

As I've developed this thesis, I have come to realize that at the heart of culture care is my desire to know the full depth of the gospel of Jesus Christ. What is the "good news"? The reductionism of our modern assumptions has caused the gospel to be truncated, limited to pragmatic and tribal concerns rather than the good news of the whole of the Bible—true life, the never-ending restoration and new creation of all things in Christ.

Culture care emphasizes that God cares for the *whole* of the creation (as his own artwork) and for history (as God's own story lived through our fallen reality), and that there is not one hair of our head or one moment of our journey that God does not pay close attention to (Luke 12:7). Culture care takes Jesus himself, who cared for people, his surroundings, and his culture, as a model for us all.

Even though culture care as a term grows out of creation care and soul care, my intended audience is wider than the Christian community. I want to speak also to those who long for beauty, to those who may not yet have recognized the need for an outward expression of Christ in their lives.

My initial reason for coming up with generative language is to translate the Spirit-filled life into terms that people outside the visible church can understand and resonate with. Even many artists who despise the church (I can name them, as they are my friends) love to speak of Jesus. I try to find a common language to speak to them about the Spirit's operation. When I do, they often recognize the Spirit, without naming him, in their studios, rehearsal halls, and poems. These observations by outsiders are critical for my understanding of culture at large; they are the grass outside of the sheepfold that feeds this sheep.

ᔕ ᔕ ᔕ

We need open gates. But we need the sheepfold too. Even for a *mearcstapa* who is skilled at living in the wider world, the welcome and safety of a sheepfold cannot be overstated. Border-stalkers need a solid grounding, a secure place to which they can return; a parabola requires a center to spin out of. The further and more powerful the parabolic movement, the stronger the center needs to be.[3]

A healthy community is one that is secure, anchored in tradition and faith, but also allowing for a dynamic movement outward, sending forth artists and missionaries, caregivers and entrepreneurs. It is centered and confident in its identity as a flock because it knows the purpose for which the Good Shepherd has gathered it: to serve and bless and transform the wider world.

Where are such healthy communities? Do any exist today? Part of our future culture care journey will be to identify communities and groups that are working to cultivate these values. We may see glimpses of the potential of what a community ought to be, but I am sure all communities suffer from lack of grace or lack of care for those in the margins. We may need to begin, therefore, by considering the cultural soil conditions; by a careful analysis, we may come up with strategies to strengthen what is healthy and compensate for factors that might compromise our vitality.

12

CULTIVATING
CULTURAL SOIL

I recently moved out of the city, and I have been gardening. I am a novice gardener, but I have realized that what I do as an artist—as a practitioner of the ancient art of Nihonga, the slow rhythm of creating a new work layer by layer over a period of time—is very similar to cultivating the right soil for my garden.

Holding soil in your hands can lead to deeper meditations on culture care.

Soil is a complex reality. Most of us do not give a thought to the fact that soil is made of decomposed dead animals, plants, and insects. I plant my seeds in what is essentially a layered mass of death, accumulated over time. Good soil also contains other things we desire as gardeners—microorganisms, worms, and nutrients that make an environment conducive for seeds to come alive.

Apply this knowledge to culture at large. Culture too is full of "dead" objects from the past. A museum is a container for such detritus, though a good museum will make it come to life in contemporary context. Today's shifting market in art and commerce is leaving behind even more layers of cultural death. The difference is that instead of past objects being reanimated in a museum, millions of cultural products now remain dormant or dead in cyberspace and in artists' studios.

If we assume, though, that winter is necessary for the spring—that death is essential for life to emerge—then our bleak and painful period is perhaps a necessary step toward the cultivation of a renewed culture. As the poet Christian Wiman puts it, "We live in and by our senses, which are conditioned in and by our deaths."[1] Cultivating—plowing, tilling—the cultural soil will loosen and aerate the various strata of earlier cultural products and ideas, making their nourishment available to new seeds and leaving our soil ready for the long-awaited thaw. When the seeds of art (and our lives) are planted in it, and the spring rains come, a culture can come alive again.

CULTURAL SOIL AND THE GOSPEL

Good soil is essential for a garden. As Jesus teaches in the parable of the sower and the soils in Matthew 13, no matter how good a seed is (and Jesus' seeds are the gospel, perfectly pristine and good), it cannot produce fruit in soil that does not allow for deep roots.

What Christians call the gospel—the good news—includes a narrative of God's work from beginning to eternity that is often summarized as creation, fall, redemption, and restoration. It begins with God's good, beautiful, and gratuitous creation, and with humankind called "very good." Humans broke away from God's purposes in Eden, and our rebellion results in ongoing fragmentation, separation, decay, and death. To redeem from death the creatures he still loves, God has acted in human history through Israel—and has come to us himself in Jesus, Israel's Messiah. When Christ returns again as he has promised, we will see the full renewal of creation and the restoration of all things toward a new creation.

What is more, if Christians are correct, the death-defeating power of Christ is active now. It operates through God's Spirit enlivening his followers. The deep life of heaven is renewing the earth. We are even now, in part, beginning to see God's will done on earth. We live now in the era in which God has invited us—more accurately, has commanded us—to participate in his creative purposes, to extend his artistry, and to contribute to the transformation of all kinds of disorder. When Jesus speaks of the seed, he is speaking toward this reintegration, the new reality breaking into our brokenness through the Spirit. It is characteristic of God's work that restoration and new creation grows from the smallest and most unlikely beginnings.

I see God as the ultimate Artist and us, still bearing God's image even in our fall, as artists writ small. The Bible is a book written by the creator God, spoken through God's creative if sometimes broken people. It is designed to recalibrate our worldview and reconnect us with God. Only then can God's power work through us as we fill—creatively and lovingly—the roles that contribute to God's work toward new creation, which is a part of the purpose for which we were made and by which we thrive.

Our current culture, often called a "culture of death," is full of pointers toward the first two gospel elements (creation and fall) but only rarely reflects, even in churches, the full story of God's love and his ongoing work toward our full thriving. I have noticed, as an artist prone to looking on from the margins, that churches often present the middle two elements (fall and redemption) but rarely connect the whole story of the Bible—that begins in creation and ends in new creation—with the stories of our present lives and communities. We often misuse this great book, reducing it to a book of rules, a checklist for earning our way into heaven, or a guidebook for material prosperity or personal well-being. Many churches replace God as Artist with God as CEO of the universe and turn to business metrics to measure their "success" at meeting his "bottom lines."

Christian communities are thus often busy with programs but rarely seen as a creative force to be reckoned with, let alone as a power of good that affects whole cities and gives everyone a song to sing. But as we more and more become gatherings of diverse people journeying together, as we learn truly to love each other with all our differences, we may help prepare the conditions in which God's good seed may bring forth new cultural life.

I see in the parable of the soils a call to a specific kind of cultural work. The new life the seed carries is beyond our capacity to provide. But we can and must contribute to the soil in which it will grow, and our efforts can affect the seed's fruitfulness. Culture care thus prepares the way for the gospel to spread.

The tilling of the soil is the most important task we can do to prepare ourselves and our culture for the seeds of the gospel that God sows so lavishly. Beauty can sometimes break through our bedrock assumptions and prepare us to consider possibilities beyond the broken wasteland of our world, just as Judy's bouquet exposed my inner pragmatism, my wasteland vision, and started my journey toward faith and thriving. Then there are the thorns—"the worries of this life and the deceitfulness of wealth"—that Jesus warns us will compete with the good seed and make it unfruitful (Matthew 13:22). Art and other culture care work can sometimes thin out such weeds, releasing the full generative potential of God's seed.

SOIL TO THRIVE IN

The God revealed in the Bible has endowed creation with overflowing beauty. This God is not characterized by utility but by abundant love.

God desires his creatures—especially those who in Christ are adopted as his children—also to be creative and generative.

As we begin as culture care gardeners, we may need to learn to think beyond our immediate context. A person who owns a backyard pond is able on one level to make decisions about her pond without consciously considering larger ecological issues. Her concern is that the pond be free of mosquitoes, but a greater scope of awareness is crucial. Morally she is responsible to learn the effects on the wider ecosystem of a pesticide that kills mosquitoes. The same process of widening our sphere of concern and anticipating the consequences or ripple effects of our actions also applies to culture.

We will not agree on every definition or approach. A dandelion is a weed to some, while to others it's part of their salad. But what is critical for our mindset is the *care* of culture. When we care for and love a parcel of land, we approach it very differently than if we simply consider it as a transactional commodity. Even if two neighbors don't see eye to eye on the use of their fields, if each truly cares for their land, they can pursue the same larger goal—to leave the land for their children and grandchildren to enjoy. We can do the same as we tend our culture, albeit in slightly different ways.

Wendell Berry, a true prophet of our time, wrote a reflection on the land promised to Abraham and his descendants, the people of Israel, for a magazine devoted to creation care. But it is applicable as much to cultural soils as to a farmer's soil:

> The difficulty but also the wonder of the story of the Promised Land is that, there, the primordial and still continuing dark story of human rapaciousness begins to be accompanied by a vein of light which, however improbably and uncertainly, still accompanies us. This light originates in the idea of the land as

a gift—not a free or a deserved gift, but a gift given upon certain rigorous conditions.[2]

Notice some of the elements revealed on the path over which Berry skillfully guides us toward wise stewardship. First, as we journey toward culture care we must recognize that we will face the "dark story of human rapaciousness." We may encounter those who value in culture only the potential for gain. We may encounter apathy and even hostility if we care about the future. But lest cynicism take over, we make our journey, as Berry points out, alongside "a vein of light." Another way to say this is that the gift given to us as makers of culture is in its nature generative. The "rigorous conditions" include our active work in tilling the soil. If the soil conditions are right, we will find our thriving.

ꙮ ꙮ ꙮ

I began my journey as an artist very early on, responding to the realization that I am built to see things differently, to question deeply the nature of reality. But today I do much more than painting. I began the efforts of International Arts Movement, and I am embarking on the core educational element of IAM, the Fujimura Institute. I have now accepted directing the Brehm Center as an extension of these efforts to steward culture and to practice being an artist in the midst of the largest Protestant seminary in the world. I have done so because as I developed as an artist and as my career grew I came to another realization: the soil of the culture in which I was planted was not soil I could thrive in. The gift of art is not allowed to grow in our highly commoditized system.

In a remarkably prescient book, *The Gift*, poet Lewis Hyde helps to explain the problem. He writes in the introduction:

It is the assumption of this book that a work of art is a gift, not a commodity. Or, to state the modern case with more precision, that works of art exist simultaneously in two "economies," a market economy and a gift economy. Only one of these is essential however: a work of art can survive without the market, but where there is no gift, there is no art.[3]

Let me borrow an analogy that Hyde uses. Before Western people came to the Pacific Northwest, Native Americans managed the salmon. They accepted salmon as a gift. They took what was necessary and trusted each year that more would come. When Westerners came and applied early modern methods to the fisheries, salmon became commodities—and the salmon population plummeted until people realized that the species must be protected from unrestrained commercial forces.

The same principle applies to the arts. The ideal conditions for the arts include a communal recognition that they are a gift to society and need some protection. The arts are a unique exception to the capitalist argument. There is nothing wrong with artists marketing their art or patrons purchasing art, but we must recognize that the arts belong primarily in the precinct of a gift economy and that artists who swim in the waters of culture need to be protected from market forces if their cultural contributions—or sometimes they themselves—are to survive.

We have seen in recent decades how care for the natural environment, like the Hudson River, has led to great renewal. Nature has its own generative power, and human stewardship can be multiplied by nature's power to restore itself. Culture, I believe, has an even greater power to restore because human gifting is already generative by nature. The human creative gift can also be powerfully healing and generative, reconciling the greatest of enemies, bridging the greatest of gaps.

It's not enough to have artists who seek after beauty, truth, and goodness; we must have churches, policies, and communities that promote a long-term nurture of culture that is beautiful, truthful, and full of goodness.

Through culture care, we need to initiate a series of models—cultural greenhouses or gardens, contained environments that allow artists to work in conditions where they can thrive, where art's gift function is recognized and valued. We need the right type of protected arenas with good gardeners to till the soil.

As I have thought about such creative microcosms, I have come to see that the image of a greenhouse is not strong enough for what is needed. Greenhouses imply a strongly sheltered environment where soil and plants are protected from the weather. They are also resource intensive, requiring careful monitoring for humidity, temperature, and other factors. And their produce, while visually appealing, often lacks in taste when compared with crops raised in the open. The garden concept is better. Open to the wind and rain, gardens are at the same time contained within walls, a planned space, with a limited scope or audience. In trying to create ideal conditions for artists, however, both greenhouse and garden concepts seem to fall into an emphasis on protection at the expense of gift to society.

Both of these models will be appropriate at times to allow new artists to take root in a dry or poisoned climate or during a frigid season, but too much time in the greenhouse is counterproductive to work that is sustainable and generative. I suspect that implementing a garden or greenhouse environment for artists is more likely to result in "Christian art" than "art from Christians." And one can already predict how unappealing such spaces would be to restless young *mearcstapas*, already primed to jump the fence.

Where is nature's most generative place? Is there a natural habitat we can emulate for artists and culture shapers that combines a reasonable amount of protection and care along with ongoing connection with the wider society? I think there is. Can culture care foster models that are challenging enough that participants will develop endurance and resilience and be prepared for generative participation and competition in the wider culture? I know it must.

13

CULTURAL ESTUARIES

*M*uch of the Hudson River, like all the intricate waterways around New York City, is an estuary. In an estuary salt water mixes with fresh, bringing together multiple ecological layers and habitats to form one of the world's most diverse and abundant ecosystems.

This abundance arises from an environment that is delicately balanced and often harsh. An environmental scientist recently told me that while an invigorated estuary contains many pockets of homogeneity—like beds of eelgrass or oysters—it is ultimately heterogeneous, for these pockets are all in contact and often in competition with each other. And each pocket is subject to the ebbs and flows of the estuarial system, including variations in salt concentration and sediment from the interaction of river and tidal waters.

Estuaries offer buffer zones for many species. They are a critical nursery area, for example, for young salmon, striped bass, and other fish that come downstream after hatching. Life in semiprotected estuarial wetlands during a critical period of their development readies these fish for life in the ocean.

Oysters are another of the many species that thrive in estuaries. They filter the water for plankton and bacteria to feed themselves, in the process serving a variety of functions critical to the health and diversity of species in the surrounding ecology. These small creatures are remarkably effective at cleaning the water they inhabit. They even turn some pollutants into pearls in the process. But they can purify some types of pollution only at the cost of polluting themselves. Because of their function as natural filters and the fact that adult oysters do not move, they are an indicator species, "canaries in the coal mines" of their ecosystems.

New York Harbor used to host oyster beds so abundant that New York City in the late 1800s was known as the world's oyster capital. But the famed oyster beds were decimated in the early 1900s by pollution and raw sewage spewing into their habitat. In 2012, when storm surges from Hurricane Sandy surprised New Yorkers, the flooding went as far up as 30th Street and destroyed many artworks in the Chelsea arts district. Had the oyster beds been intact, some say, the natural seawall they formed would have mitigated Sandy's damage, so restoring the oyster beds is one of the poststorm responses under consideration. I lost fifty-five precious works that day at Dillon Gallery, located in the west side of Chelsea, in the surge of waters. As Providence would have it, that Tuesday I was to truck in new works, a series ironically called "Walking on Water." I was fortunate that these new works were safe in my Princeton studio. Would the oyster beds have prevented such an unthinkable demise of Chelsea galleries—demise that many did not recover from?

ဢ ဢ ဢ

Estuaries offer a key model for culture care. We can think of the river of culture as an estuary, a complex system with a multiplicity of dynamic influences and tributaries. Within it are many nurturing—but not isolated—habitats. Their purpose is not so much *protection* as *preparation*. Each individual habitat strengthens its participants to interact with the wider environment, making for a diversity that is healthy enough for true competition. Connected habitats allow for exposure to stronger currents, which push participants to build stronger swimming muscles or grow deeper roots, depending on the context, strengthening each for the overall flourishing of the greater cultural ecology.

Understanding cultural communities in this framework reduces the pressure for strict categorization and rigid programming and helps us better serve diverse populations. We might consider some artists and creative catalysts as oysters of the cultural estuary, rooted and making life better around them. Others may be more like salmon, spending only a season in a nurturing habitat before heading out to sea or making their contribution to life upstream. Some of those passing through will return to the estuary, while others may not.

The point is that different callings require different habitats and different types of care; no single agenda or program can serve them all, but all can contribute to the flourishing of the estuary and to the wider environment. In this model, culture care happens best in a condition of vigorous diversity and healthy but rigorous competition, responsive to cultural currents. True diversity moves beyond mere tolerance to respect for the other in the context of our common life. Just as natural estuaries are highly delicate, we also need a macro vision for stewardship that cares for the overall system and respects many types of contributions.

The action of oysters in filtering the water around them—with the byproduct of turning irritants into iridescence—is part of the way a diverse ecosystem can regenerate toward sustainability. But beauty is far more than a byproduct. And culture is far more than sustainable—it is generative by nature. Artists and creative catalysts gathered together may also contribute to larger structures that can serve as a seawall or breakwater against the currents of utilitarianism and commodification that erode our humanity.

There are historical examples of such cultural estuaries. Sixteenth-century Japan, which produced many art forms, including Sen-no-Rikyu, the distinctive vision of tea, became a fantastic cultural estuary as Portuguese and Italian missionaries came into a land of feudal struggles. Early twentieth-century New York City, with exiles coming in from threats abroad and American struggles in the South, created a mixture of influences that birthed abstract expressionism and the Harlem Renaissance. Pre-Renaissance Europe, with Ottoman invasions bringing a mixture of Islamic and Asian cultures into contact with the West, is another example, as are the salons of Paris in the eighteenth and nineteenth centuries.

While this book can offer only a gesture toward identifying and learning from these examples, it will be a worthwhile journey for social scientists and historians to come together to study such past examples for lessons to be applied to culture care. Among the questions worth asking: What degrees of cultural buffering and exposure are helpful at different stages of personal and communal growth? Can we find ways to keep our "oysters" healthy as they help filter cultural pollution? What connections are beneficial between kindred habitats? What critical mass makes for a generative habitat?

❧ ❧ ❧

Understanding what we do from historical examples, what can we begin to do today? Culture care begins with generative practice in our everyday lives. We need to create cultural estuaries, each abundant with diversity and providing safe harbor for the creatives journeying through them. Generative practices grow from generative principles. Are our communities open to different expressions of leadership and vision to guide us in the current cultural flux? Are we confident enough in our identities to open the gates to wider cultural pastures? Are we keeping our soil cultivated for growth?

Let's return to our discussion of border-stalkers. Most potential *mearcstapas* start within a community, however close or strained their ties. What might have happened if Emily Dickinson had been affirmed in her idiosyncratic path, had found in life the support that her poems found nearly a century later? What if Vincent van Gogh had found in his church a safe environment to pursue his creativity?

These fanciful questions have no direct answers, as the context of these artists' lives and decisions create a complex matrix of possibilities. Yet their examples are certainly worth pondering as we ask what, practically, a church or community should do when someone like Vincent or Emily—or like C.J.—is in its midst. How do we support artists to act generatively rather than transgressively? Let me sketch out an initial response here. We can deputize them, then form, train, commission, and support them.

First, we can deputize potential *mearcstapas*. We can teach all the members of the community about this role, and then the community can identify potential border-stalkers as they are raised up or welcomed into the community. If we can recognize them earlier in their own development, we can make space for them to grow within and between our normal, comfortable categories and provide consistent care for them as they discern their calling.

Second, we can provide a nurturing environment with a degree of structure or intentionality, in which artists can be trained in the skills necessary for their new roles. This would include a grounding in the "tribal" or group identity, a critical formation. We can provide soul care opportunities, spiritual and artistic weight rooms that will militate against isolation and alienation and give artists resources for their journeys. We can help them develop and live out their faith identity as noun rather than adjective. We can create places and opportunities for artists to interact with each other inside the community. This might include mentorships, apprenticeships, and regular ongoing opportunities for unstructured connections. All of this will provide context for interactions that will happen concurrently and subsequently outside the community.

Third, we can provide training and practice in exploring the boundaries, interacting with other groups, moving in and out of different identities, finding news of cultural pasturage to be carried back to the community. This might be a more guided exercise in the beginning and a more independent one as individuals grow. We can be encouraging as they come to value the messy areas of tribal conflict, learn new vocabularies and ways of thinking, and begin to report back. We can also affirm these future leaders in developing their skills in generosity and loving the unlovable, helping them call us to remember the poor to whom we are called to bring good news.

Fourth, the community may want at some point to commission its apprentice or journeyman *mearcstapas* for their next role: moving into the wastelands, the oceans, or wherever they are called.

Finally, the community can provide ongoing support—moral, practical, and financial. For artists who stay near their original community, that should go without saying. But those *mearcstapas* who move on should be encouraged to form and maintain connections with other local communities wherever they go, contributing to the life in their new space as well as sending or bringing back news to their commissioning community.

The details of this approach will need to be filled in (I give a few more suggestions in the following chapters), but this model does offer a way to release the full generative efforts of these creatives, who can offer much to our churches and communities and the wider culture. They can cast the appealing vision of beauty in the face of injustice, revealing brokenness and need, modeling love for the unlovable, revealing complexities, brokering reconciliation, teaching us to speak appealingly and persuasively, guiding the whole community through the challenges of engaging with the culture, leading us away from fragmentation and onward toward reintegration, and—perhaps—even uncovering again the Spirit's light in the churches.

14

CUSTODIANS OF
CULTURE CARE

*I*n a culture such as ours, bringing home a bouquet of flowers can be a transgressive act. I want here to write of someone who is not an artist and offer a real-life parable on the Hudson River estuary.

In the early 1960s, Fred Danback came home from the Korean War to work at Anaconda Wire and Cable, a copper wire factory in Hastings-on-Hudson, New York, thirty miles north of Manhattan. It was a booming enterprise. But he soon became troubled by what he saw at the factory. To restore beauty to the river he had grown up with, Danback became a whistleblower against his own company.

In a PBS interview with Bill Moyers, Danback said, "I seen all kinds of oil and sulfuric acid, copper filings; my gosh, they were coming out of that company like it was going out of style." He said that shad fishermen started to lose "their business because there was oil in the water that would cause the fish to be contaminated with it, and the Fulton Market refused to take their weekly catch. . . . [Anaconda] and other businesses were polluting a river and hurting a second business, the shad fishermen. I didn't think they had the right to do that. It used to really infuriate me. I became obsessed with fighting pollution."[1]

Fred complained to the company's managers about his fisherman friends' plight. Each time he did, it seemed, he got demoted. He ended up as a custodian. But Fred never gave up. He worked in that custodian role, literally pushing his broom into every room of the company. He also took copious notes and made maps of the company. What was intended as a punishment ended up as the best possible opportunity to spy on the company. He had all the keys!

There were few pollution laws at the time. Fred and a few other pioneers of the environmental movement decided to sue Anaconda under an archaic law called the Refuse Act of 1899, which Fred found out about while cleaning the local library. In 1972, when the US Attorney's Office found a way to prosecute Anaconda, they used Fred's maps and notes as evidence.

"The company was fined $200,000 under the Refuse Act of 1899, you know. . . . Even today for a polluter to be fined $200,000 is a big event. Back in the early 1970s, it was a huge event. It was like a thunderclap," said Fred later. Today, three million striped bass go up and down the Hudson because Fred's efforts led to changes in the laws of the land.

∽   ∽   ∽

I draw three lessons for culture care from this story: we need to be willing to sacrifice, we need to remember our first love, and we need to be taking copious notes.

First, culture care requires sacrifice. We need to be willing to endure demotions, becoming "custodians" of culture care. By being demoted for the right reasons, however, we may gain a humble authority, which can work like keys to unlock doors of cultural "factories," giving us opportunities to clean up—and to see what is really going on. Our keys are humility, integrity, determination, and hope for things to come. In the current art world in which ego, selfishness, and self-destructiveness abound, we will stand out, eventually, if we have an ounce of human decency and generosity. What if we are willing to serve someone rather than do art for self-expression? What if we collaborated in humility and gave ourselves in service, not expecting the world, or our audience, to agree with us or applaud us?

Second, we need to remember our first love. Bill Moyers asked Fred Danback, "What kept you going?" Danback replied, "I love that river. It's a beautiful river. Look at it. It's your river, it's my river; it belongs to everybody. Who's got a right to mess it up? That's the way I feel about it. I still do, to this day." His memory of that beautiful river kept him going through a long struggle.

What keeps us going? Do we keep our first love—the reason we became artists in the first place—in focus, or have we become distracted by the need for survival? Your first love as an artist may have been revealed when you drew something on paper that came alive to you. Or perhaps you were playing a character in a school play and you realized that you had entered another person's world, a world you never knew existed. Or perhaps as a dancer you made a single leap that seemed to defy gravity. A first love for creative catalysts may have been when a song began to burn deep within you as a teen, or when you encountered a painting that you had to keep going back to, as something in that work kept opening up new vistas for you.

One way to approach the rediscovery of our first love may be by considering the contrast—what is now causing you to lose hope? Because artists and creative folks are gifted receptors, sensitive to the world's woes, we may be the first to internalize problems and be in despair. It is through this first love that we can recognize what is not supposed to be. If we forget it, we will end up being swallowed in the polluted river and lose our vision for making art—and possibly for living.

Third, we need to take copious notes. Just like Fred Danback, we need to fulfill our responsibilities as custodians of culture—cleaning where we can. We can use our new keys to unlock the workrooms of cultural production. We can take notes to show people the flawed practices that flow out as cultural pollutants, so these can be identified and addressed. Fred was not an artist, but many readers of this book are. Our notebooks should be filled with drawings, with color and fantastic designs. We are gifted with creativity and expression. Our notes should be beautiful, good, and true.

Stewardship of culture and stewardship of nature go side by side. The activities of the arts are acts of stewardship. Many people see the arts and entertainment as enemies, or at least view them with healthy suspicion, and not without cause. Many recent expressions of the arts have twisted the good, the true, and the beautiful in the same way that we have polluted our rivers. The arts are always upstream of culture, and artists are the creators of culture. The question is, how do we enact change?

ᔕ ᔕ ᔕ

There's not a day that I do not think of Fred Danback. As I used to jog on the promenade of the river, I thanked God for Fred's sowing the initial seeds of sacrifice. As I follow the bluebirds' nesting behavior at my farmland now, I think of his work to create cleaner rivers and air. But there's more to the story.

As the horrific news began to come out about the airliner attacks of September 11, 2001, the initial estimate of those who perished was twelve to fifteen thousand. In the next few days, however, the numbers kept decreasing, eventually to 2,977—still unbearable, surely. I have a theory about why the initial estimate turned out to be so wrong.

September 11 was the first day of school. There were eight thousand students around the World Trade Center towers. Parents had just dropped off their children—as did my wife with our three—when the sinister shadow of the first plane passed over them in the schoolyard. Few of those parents made it to work. Those who did came back down the steps right away, like many of our friends, ignoring the fatal direction to "stay where you are."

You may not yet see the connection with Fred Danback, but there is a direct link in my mind. Here it is: all of the schools around the towers were built since the late 1970s. Because Danback was willing to be demoted, the river became cleaner. Because the river became cleaner, the parks around the river became attractive. Because the parks were good, young couples becoming parents decided to stay in their small Battery Park apartments instead of escaping to suburbia. Because of the resulting tremendous increase in the student population starting in the late seventies, the city built all those schools.

I am convinced Fred Danback made a difference on 9/11. One person with the courage to be demoted, one person willing to sacrifice for the restoration of beauty, created a ripple effect in culture with immeasurable generative influence. The effects of his action cannot be measured but can be told only in how we live our lives—and so it is worth noting that the children of 9/11, including our three, grew up to be enormously resilient, creative, and community minded.

Culture care actions, similarly, cannot be measured by typical metrics of effectiveness and efficiency. The measure of success must be in how our sacrifice to make culture care possible manifests itself in the lives of our children.

☙ ☙ ☙

We need to become a community of Fred Danbacks. We should never forget the beauty of the river of our calling, and we should have the courage to speak and sacrifice on its behalf.

People like Danback awoke us to the beauty of the Hudson River. We no longer see a black river as a good thing or as the inevitable result of progress. Something shifted in culture on the environmental front, and we need to replicate that shift with culture itself, with the rivers of culture that are now also blackened and uninhabitable with utilitarian pragmatism and over-commodification.

We need not be opposed to industry or capitalism to be culture care agents. The problems we face arise not from producing copper wires or being involved in profitable businesses but from a narrowing of our understanding of success to only what is measurable with consumption and utility—and ultimately from a failure of care and courage.

15

BUSINESS CARE

*T*he model of the cultural estuary—a heterogeneous, competitive environment that is preserved toward a thriving culture—applies, in fact, equally to capitalistic ventures, entrepreneurism, and what I have begun to call *business care*. Healthy capitalistic competition can also be conducive for the growth of culture. It may be useful to begin this discussion by further defining the term *creative catalysts* as a key ingredient toward culture care.

Creative catalysts are those who may not be full-time artists but desire to contribute to creating an enduring shift in the culture of their chosen fields. Catalysts are, by definition, elements that serve generative growth by being present in the mixture of a microcosm. A creative catalyst could be a business CEO, a teacher, a custodian, or even an artist who goes beyond self-expression.

A CREATIVE CATALYST IN ACTION

A former board member of International Arts Movement, David Fuller, is a fine example of a creative catalyst. As a bank executive, he at first felt out of place attending one of our conferences. But in one of the lectures, he heard another business leader speak of being a "creative catalyst" and helping to "rehumanize" the culture of business around us.

Dave returned from this arts conference and convened a discussion at his Oklahoma City bank. He gathered the bank's owners and senior management and led them in asking two questions: (1) How can we as a bank be "rehumanized"? and (2) As a for-profit company, how can we have multiple bottom lines that *care* for our community? Dave recently wrote me an email recounting this journey:

> We established what we called a Team Fund. It was partially funded by the bank, by individual contributions, and through projects like "Jeans Days." Each Friday, employees can wear jeans if they contribute $3 to the Team Fund. The employees at each location decide how money in that fund is used. One day a young mom with two kids in the car came through the drive-thru of one of our small rural locations. Her car died and wouldn't start. Her battery was dead. A couple of our employees pushed her car to the parking lot. Then, with money from their Team Fund, they bought a new battery and installed it for her. It sounds simple but was so profound on many levels.

A creative catalyst modeling and extending rehumanized values created a culture care condition. In the ripple effect from one leader, a bank ended up taking care of a single mom in need of help. This single, collaborative act of generosity called for creativity and imagination from both workers and management. This one act has already begun to multiply generatively into the bank's culture, increasing awareness, communication, and loyalty to (and from) customers.

Often business practice and art making are seen as things at opposing poles on a spectrum of pragmatics and creativity. On one hand, business discipline requires convergent decision making, narrowing down to a particular focus and a bottom line in a highly organized system. Such a mindset can provide stability to the system, and it has been a dominant force in our culture. Artists, on the other hand, are divergent thinkers, often seem to thrive on uncertainty, and are resourceful enough to survive on very little.

Business care, as an extension of culture care, creates a hybrid microcosm, merging business and art. In addition, we have learned at IAM that a significant contribution can be made to any growing organization, whether it be a business or church, if the pragmatic decision makers *invite* artists to participate in the decision-making process—if analytical thinkers intentionally involve intuitive thinkers. Dave did that by bringing the word *rehumanize* to the context of his bank's decision making.

I recently had lunch with a business leader. We shared what people are faced with today in our areas of expertise, so I naturally shared a bit about the plight of artists. I then asked him what his clients, who are CEOs and bankers, are facing. He spoke of how bankers, after the Lehman Brothers collapse, now have to justify their work. Many bankers became bankers for stability and high income; they are willing to work hard for that, but they previously never had to justify their choice. But now bankers asked "what do you do?" at a party will have to defend their continuing in that profession. He said that this is also true of some CEOs.

I am used to defending my decision to be an artist in this pragmatic world. If a banker now has to do the same thing, it occurred to me that a banker and an artist can now have a more meaningful discussion on how they can help each other toward thriving and a vision for a rehumanized culture. In such a conversation, the language of care—for both business and culture—is not only desired but necessary for all people. We are facing an inflection point in culture that demands more than bottom-line thinking. We need business care.

I am often asked, "How does one create a movement?" In order to start a movement, you need three elements: (1) An artist type with creative capital, (2) a pastor or community organizer type with social capital, and (3) a business type with access to material capital. To illustrate the point when I share this idea with others, I draw a triangle such as the one shown here.

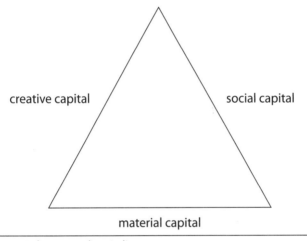

Figure 1.1. Rehumanized capitalism

What is interesting about this triangle is that if you have two out of the three, you can make what you do sustainable. For instance, if you are creative and have an abundance of funding, you can continue to create. If you have many friends and are very creative, you will do fine too. But if you only have one out of three, you are in trouble. Imagine a rich person with no creativity and no friends.

Since most of us are not gifted with all three, we will need to partner with those who are different from us. A cultural estuary will likely provide people who are different from us, and we need to begin befriending outside of our area of comfort.

So I encourage someone who wants to begin a culture care movement in their region to gather a core group with all three of these types of capital. If you are an artist, find a pastor friend and a business entrepreneur. Two out of three will make what you do sustainable; three out of three can launch a generative movement to which you can invite others.

16

PRACTICAL ADVICE
FOR ARTISTS

*M*any artists struggle to make a living from their work, and I am often asked how I began my career. I answer first by speaking of the mindset I have found essential. Being self-supporting is good, but it is also a noble thing to be able to work nine-to-five in an unrelated field—even in a boring job—when this is done purposefully to make art possible. If you are waiting tables, it's one thing to do so to pay your rent, but it is another thing entirely to do so to make your art. In the former mindset you are in survival mode, barely making it; in the latter you are always creating, letting your intuition germinate, even as you serve others. This is the generative path.

Many masterpieces of still life paintings from seventeenth- and eighteenth-century Amsterdam (the golden age of Dutch painting) were produced by shopkeepers who sold cheese until early afternoon, then closed up shop and painted for the rest of the day. T. S. Eliot was a banker, Wallace Stevens an insurance salesman, Dana Gioia a marketing executive. These and other notable writers and artists have had day jobs. Some have told me that they create better when they have a stable work environment. Others even look intentionally for boring bureaucratic work.

Are you called to make art? Make sure to ask this question with a few advisers. It's a good idea, a friend once told my son, to have a "board of directors" for your life. This accountability group should be people you trust—and who can tell you the truth. They can be peers or elder sages, but they should include people with expertise you lack, such as lawyers, accountants, or entrepreneurs. You should also include people with experience in the arts who can help you discern your true calling—or its absence.

It is impossible to be an artist today. You must persevere beyond your limits, facing naysayers, your doubts, and your limited abilities. But if painting—or acting, or writing—is the only way you will find your inner thriving, then you must cultivate that art and see whether your work can lead to thriving for both you and your family. Under such conditions, if you are not deeply convinced of your call, vacillation will cause despair and affect your work.

RAISING SUPPORT

After graduating from college, I knew that I needed to try to make it as an artist. Even though I was not a Christian at the time, I often used the expression "I am called" to describe the inner sense that I had to try to develop my art. I looked for a job that allowed me to paint part time. I was fortunate to find an assistant teaching position in a local special education school. The story of Judy bringing home a bouquet of flowers occurred at that time. Even my failure to be an artist then turned out, in the long run, to be a generative experience.

Later on, when I discovered that it was Christ who was calling me, it occurred to me that he would also care about me enough to supply my needs and those of my family. Christ reveals an infinite God, and he commands us to "seek first his kingdom and his righteousness, and all these things will be given to you as well"

(Matthew 6:33). I have come to recognize that God does not promise an easy path but an abundant path.

I found myself in a community of missionaries who helped me to understand my new journey as a Christian. I became convinced that God had called me back into the arts after my transfer of allegiance to Christ. I was sure of my calling, and my missionary friends seemed sure of theirs. So I asked them, "How do you make your calling sustainable?" They told me that they raised support. They went around to all their friends and contacts, as well as many churches, and let them know of their call to be missionaries in Japan. In the process they sharpened their articulation of their calling and tested that sense of calling.

I was a graduate student, with a wife and a child now. I thought, *Well, I am called to be an artist, so how do we apply this to my art?* I had a few successful shows—which means a few pieces sold and I had a good review in the *Japan Times*—and several people became interested in my work and visited me in my studio. I began to ask whether they would be willing to support me as an artist for a year. I asked them not to pay me up front to purchase a piece but to pay in monthly installments. I figured this would help me to learn to budget, and it turned out to be so. Soon I had six or seven people willing to do this, paying, for example, $100 a month and coming to the studio at the end of the year to pick a work worth $1,200. Combined with my scholarship, I was able to sustain a living with my art even as a graduate student.

I then went to a gallery interested in my work and told them that I wanted to do a show, but that half of the works in the exhibit would already have been sold due to this arrangement. I told the gallery that having half of the paintings sold, with red dots next to them, as the show opened would give the exhibit momentum. They agreed. This is how I got my start. It came out of my need to support my family, but even today what I do is based on the same model.

Most of the collectors who first purchased my works were Japanese "salary men." They were not wealthy, but they loved art. Many of them supported me for the duration of my stay in Japan and then donated the works they bought to museums. I was very fortunate. None of the collectors in the first ten years of my career were "Christian" collectors.

THREE GS FOR ARTISTS

More recently, in moving toward culture care I have come to realize that it's beneficial to think and pray not just toward sustainability but toward generativity. Let's apply the three Gs at an individual level.

Genesis moments. Every moment can be a genesis moment, and artists are often attuned to this reality more than most. A visit by a collector to a studio can be an opportunity to serve the collector and create such moments. A generatively focused collector will likely be more interested in learning from the creative process and helping the artist toward thriving.

Of course, the art market includes galleries and even collectors who treat art as strict transaction. I try to avoid both (which means I am limiting my career quite a bit). I consider it a privilege when people visit my studio or an exhibit to purchase a painting. My prayer is that my art will continue to create genesis moments in their lives.

It may also help to consider the potential for genesis moments as a point of perspective when speaking with potential purchasers. People balk at buying art that is, let's say, $1,200. It seems like a lot of money, and it is a sacrifice to most people. It is also only $100 a month—approaching the price of a movie outing for a family of five. A movie seen with your family is memorable but ephemeral. An artwork you own can provide years of genesis moments in your own home, and you are investing in generativity as well by helping an artist continue her work.

Generosity. I've found that artists can be the most generous people in the world. When we hold auctions or other fund requests for IAM, it is always the artists who send in their works (framed and ready for hanging), show up to volunteer, and even send checks. One time we received a check for five dollars from an artist. I knew that this was a great sacrifice for her, and I had tears in my eyes as I thanked her. She said she was ashamed by the amount, but I assured her that her gesture meant more to the staff than she realized. Artists need to lead in generosity in society and in the church, for they are in regular touch with the gratuity of the created order. God created gratuitously, and so can we.

Generational. The arts are generative by nature, so people regardless of their faith dispositions find themselves thinking generationally. At any good museum you will see works from five hundred years ago— Fra Angelicos and Michelangelos, da Vincis and Raphaels. Have you ever thought that somehow what you do or make can last five hundred years? It is possible but unlikely that our works will be known that long from now. But a faithful community stewarding culture will mean the creation of many works of art that will inspire future generations to create toward that five-hundred-year vision. What you make now may be done to prepare the foundation for your children and subsequent generations to find thriving. This may cost you status or success, but some art could be a sacrificial offering toward future thriving.

If you are a supporter of the arts, try fitting what you do into this five-hundred-year quest as well. Your small investment today to help an artist, a dancer, or a theater group could be a stone thrown into the pond of culture, its ripple effect more substantial than your own immediate experience.

◯ ◯ ◯

At an artist talk at my gallery in the 1990s, I complained about the fact that most of the collectors who purchased the works I made in response to God's call were non-Christians. I said that since I was creating art as a calling, I wanted some of my works to go to Christians' homes. A Philadelphia pastor was in the audience. He became the first pastor to purchase one of my prints. I knew that he was sacrificing to commit to this, and something of a weight fell from my shoulders as I heard it. I felt affirmed in my calling. That pastor is now the president of a major Christian college. Every time I think of my calling, I think of his act and how much his single purchase encouraged me.

Attitude matters. Even if you are truly called, you will find occasions to complain when circumstances do not align with that sense of call. This is different from an attitude of entitlement that is enraged when the world does not instantly support you (I avoid the work of young artists with such a view). But a complaint coming out of your calling is more invitation than demand. As I spoke of a lack of Christian collectors in my life, I was smiling, and I remember it being less a demand than a prayer.

Having a positive outlook in adversity should be one of the main factors you consider in recognizing your calling. Rather than giving up because of the many, many closed doors we face as artists, and rather than being angry at the world for "our art not meeting the needs of the world," we can rejoice in our lack, as it is ultimately God, the grand Artist, who will answer our cry and provide bread for our journey.

"Blessed are those who are persecuted because of righteousness," says Jesus in Matthew 5:10. He is speaking to artists as much as any other group of his followers. An artist is called by God just as much as any missionary or church member. All of us, artists and others alike, will face some degree of struggle in responding to our call. But we are all called into love, and we need to be bold in declaring our calls. For artists who create through such a calling toward a greater love, art is at the core of their reality, their very existence. Just as Emily Dickinson had to write, as Vincent van Gogh had to paint, as Mahalia Jackson had to sing, so must we journey on to create a greater condition of awareness, a new vista of care for all.

17

TILLING OUR CULTURAL SOIL
IN THE AGE OF ANXIETY

In the summer of 2011, a Japanese farmer planted sunflower seeds in the tainted soil of Fukushima, a few miles away from the earthquake-damaged Daiei nuclear facilities. The radioactive leakage had continued since the devastating tsunami on March 11, 2011. Why would he do that? It's because he learned that sunflowers have a unique ability to take up radioactive isotopes and store them in their seeds. The farmer would harvest the flowers, which contained pods of radioactivity, making the earth less polluted.

What if our cultural soil too is tainted beyond repair? Would any efforts to till it be worthwhile at all? These questions have swirled in my mind as I wrote *Culture Care*. Some people have considered our culture to be a "culture of death" and believed that our cultural soil, just like in Fukushima, is a wasteland.

This story of the sunflower farmer tells us that even if the soil is radioactive, we still need to be farmers.

❧ ❧ ❧

When I lectured on culture care in Michigan, a Muslim woman scholar came up to me afterward and shared her tears with me. "In my country, culture wars literally mean life or death. Thank you for your thesis: culture care may save lives."

When I began to lecture on this thesis, I never imagined that culture care could save lives. But when I consider the plight of the culture this woman comes from, I realize she is right. Further, with the scope of American influence today, culture wars rhetoric can lead to literal wars. In such a polarized condition we need to create another path toward a conversation of diversity and plurality.

Culture care agents nurture the good, true, and beautiful into the soil of culture. Reinhold Niebuhr stated that "democracy is a method of finding proximate solutions to insoluble problems."[1] The growth of democracy requires good cultural soil so that "proximate solutions" can further the privilege of stewarding culture. The goal is not to win at all costs—democracy never claims to resolve insoluble problems of complex pluralism, no matter who the leader is. Niebuhr also warns us, "Nothing which is true or beautiful or good makes complete sense in any immediate context of history; therefore we must be saved by faith."[2] Culture care is generational work, and it will require much faith.

Dr. Martin Luther King Jr., the day before he was shot to death in Memphis, gave a stirring address now known as his "Mountaintop Speech." In it he stated, "Men, for years now, have been talking about war and peace. But now, no longer can they just talk about it. It is no longer a choice between violence and nonviolence in this world; it's nonviolence or nonexistence. That is where we are today."[3]

What does it mean to say "I have a dream today" in the midst of such a radioactive, anxiety-filled culture? We must remember Dr. King's admonition to note that it is "no longer a choice between violence and nonviolence" but "it's nonviolence or nonexistence." As the Muslim scholar reminded me, this non-choice is a dire reality. No longer a luxurious nonessential, culture care is the only way forward to sow seeds of hope into the arid and tainted soils of our day.

Indeed, to say "I have a dream today" is to plant seeds of hope in the radioactive soil of disappointments, fears, and trauma.

When we "win" culture war battles by demonizing the other side, the resulting paralysis and disappointments lead to the expanse of fissures rather than the soil of abundance. Having deep convictions about the world is important; but the problem is in assuming that there is a zero-sum environment in which someone wins and someone loses. Cultural estuaries thrive on diversity. Therefore, convictions resulting in sharp disagreements are not the problem. Seeing an environment of severely limited resources, in fear believing that the soil of culture can no longer be a place of abundance, and being trapped in that fear is the problem.

A culture of fear has never produced great culture. We do not create great art in response to fear and anxiety; we create great art by loving culture, loving the materials and stories from which to create art. We create great art by having faith to love our neighbors as ourselves and even love our enemies. We must remember that a cultural estuary is a heterogeneous environment. As we journey through the polarized culture, even if we cannot find common ground we can still find a way to value differences and to heed the call to love. "Common life," a term used in the subtitle of this book, is different from "common ground." "Common life" assumes pluralistic diversity and yet affirms that these differences can be a basis of an abundant cultural estuary. Caring rejuvenates culture by aspiring to the greater good, actively mediating and guiding people through the darkness of injustice.

To nurture the soil of culture, we must learn to see with the eyes of our hearts (Ephesians 1:18), beyond fear, beyond anxiety, and beyond despair. Be patient and longsuffering, especially in the midst of diversity; love deeply through these differences; nurture the soil of imagination that seeks to understand the other, gestating in faith until we can give birth to a city of "our better angels," as Abraham Lincoln put it. What if we did that? We would find a city filled with the aroma of the new, emanating out of the extravagant, with denizens like bright sunflowers turning their heads toward the sun. Out of the trauma of our times and the disillusionment of our days, God would birth something true, good, and beautiful. And God may yet purify our soils from the radioactive poison of fear in the age of anxiety.

W. H. Vanstone, an Anglican theologian, noted in *Love's Endeavour, Love's Expense*, after watching craftsman work to create: "Therefore, through this simple incident, I was helped to see that awareness of the importance of any aspect of material reality may be awareness not of its relevance to human well-being but simply of its being the work of love, and that a sense of responsibility for it may be a sense of responsibility for a work of love."[4]

Culture care is this "work of love" of the soil of culture. It may be that we need to protect our land from invaders, but it is certainly true that if we do not cultivate our soil of culture with love, we will not have anything fruitful to make it worthwhile to invade. If the cultural soil is abundant with fruit, the land may be able to provide more than sustainable food for our bodies—it may yet provide generative food for our souls so that we can invite even strangers and enemies to the table as well (Psalm 23).

A PARABLE OF BEES

I stood there with bees buzzing all about me. "Don't let a bee crawl into your ear," one of the beekeepers said. "Flick it out if they do because they will not get out of there."

I was one of about twenty-five students in a Rutgers University extension beginner's beekeeping class ("Beeginner's Class") at their ecological center. After a morning session describing honey bee types (seven), behavior, and basics of bee ecology (a very complex sociobiology in colonies), the beekeeper said suddenly, "Okay, it's time to go and observe the hives."

Bob the beekeeper said, "If you are wearing a wool sweater, take that off, because bees can get tangled in them. If you are really afraid, then stand back because they will sense your fear." We followed the beekeepers out into a cold fall day in New Jersey, and about halfway to the hives I realized that we were wearing no protective covers over our bodies and no mesh face and head covers. Beekeepers just kept leading us to the top of the hill where the hive boxes were. I felt like a child camper being encouraged by enthused teen counselors to jump into a cold lake.

I stood halfway between fearful students and the mound of beehives up the hill. I was not as bold as some students, but I did find the patterns of bees swarming to be quite beautiful when Bob opened the box. After he showed us how to use the smoker, the smoke from pine needles was pungent in the air. I was close enough to see Bob grab one of the bees crawling on his hand and squeeze it intentionally to make it sting him. The bee squirmed, and its tail snapped into Bob's suntanned skin. He let the bee fall to the ground and motioned us to come closer. "See that sack pulsating?"

Yes, there was a sack, the white glistening triangular remains like a tiny heart attached to the stinger. Bees die when they sting, so they do not like to sting unless provoked, we learned.

"I have forty-five seconds," Bill said. "All you have to do is to flick the sack off." Bill flicked the sack with his index fingernail like it was a speck of dust. "The toxins will not go into your body if you do that."

All of us nodded, still a bit skeptical that bees are as harmless as they seemed to Bob.

Bees do check you out, as you are part of their morning duties of inspecting their environs. As several of them crawled on my hands (I did imagine one crawling into my ear, but they did not), I had a revelation.

Artists are like bees.

Artists sting, or at least have the reputation that they sting. In various communities, including churches, artists have a reputation of being hard to deal with and even toxic to the group. We are also curious creatures, buzzing about the neighborhood, checking out crevices to seek out beauty in unexpected places. Artists (*mearcstapas*) in such a search may seem rather strange, even dangerous. People look for protective gear when they enter museums, especially the contemporary wing. Most artists do not want to sting, but they are intuitive explorers, and they can sense your fears.

We all need to learn from honeybees and beekeepers. Our ecosystem is in dire need of bees. The hive collapse syndrome has spread (due to bee mites, according to the beekeepers), and without bee pollination, fruit and vegetable production will be severely limited. In the California almond industry alone 1.6 million bee colonies are imported from other states to ensure the pollination of almond flowers. Bill was one of those exporters, raising bees to truck to Florida and California for pollination seasons.

Cultural fields are also in dire need of pollination. Artists are pollinators of culture, and culture cannot produce flowers without artists' efforts.

Where there are good culture care keepers, artists may simply be allowed to roam freely to pollinate. Many assume that artists have stingers and stay away, intentionally isolating artists in their community as a result. But artists are essential for the culture at large, and the artists I know do not want to sting anyone.

Artists have been secluded from the working realities of most people's lives, and art (especially with a capital "A," in the "high art" circles) has become an elitist activity. We have sequestered artists to a limited area of influence; it is time we release them to wider pastures. Because of the polarized reality resulting from many years of culture wars, we also have a "hive collapse" with artists not being able to sustain their living or to create a future generation of arts leaders.

Honeybees can pollinate flowers up to 2.5 miles from their hives. Many sociobiology studies have been done on working bees coming back to the hive to communicate the location of the flowers to the other bees with a complex series of dances. *Mearcstapas*, artists border-stalking in the field of culture, also send scouts to the furthest reaches of cultures, and perhaps even create complex series of dances and art to communicate where the cultural nectars are.

Bees excrete, out of their exploration, honey; sweet and tasty, honey also preserves and rarely spoils. Such a delectable result is the produce of a cultural estuary. Can our art too become an enduring nectar drawn from our border-stalking journeys? What if our art fed many hungry or bitter souls as part of God's good plan to nurture and preserve us? Such is the journey of culture care.

18

NEW VOCABULARIES, NEW STORIES

The overall strategy of culture care is to create cultural estuaries. Our reading groups, churches, and schools can become microcosms of care. The discussion guide at the end of this book was developed by two early implementers, Julie Silander and Peter Edman, to help these groups. All can participate in the process. As we are seeing, before we can begin to create such harbors, we will have to reexamine some conventionally held cultural viewpoints and inject new vocabulary into our dialogues, moving away from culture wars to culture care. Let me end with an example.

On a visit to Biola University, I spoke with a photographer who had graduated from Biola's art department. She creates works of art and also uses her craft as a wedding photographer to make a living. As we discussed culture care, we agreed that the phrase "taking a photograph" is problematic. When we take a photograph, what exactly are we doing? Are we taking that person's image as some characters in the movie *Lawrence of Arabia* thought of photographs— like stealing a person's soul?

The paparazzi's taking of celebrity photos for commercial gain or for the sheer excitement of exposing a scandalous moment seems indeed to take away someone's soul, treating the subject as somehow more thing than human. Might not this contribute to the way many celebrity actors and musicians seem to get caught in a drained and zombie-like existence, desensitized and alienated from their own natural gifts that should be conveying to others a deep, embedded sense of humanity? Photographic taking also accentuates a culture-wars mindset of manipulating images to amplify the divide.

This photographer and I arrived together at a fine alternative. What if we "gifted" photographs instead of "taking" them? Might it be possible to practice photography as a gift to the person at whom one points the camera? How might a commercial photographer modify the transactional nature of that work to make a living and, even better, be generative? This may seem to be a simple, even innocent, approach. But words are powerful. The mindset going into a shoot and how we speak about photographs can be, just like Scout's intervention in *To Kill a Mockingbird*, both prophetic and innocent at the same time.

We are attempting to contribute to this type of reimagining at International Arts Movement. At the Brehm Center, we train creative students to integrate their theological, spiritual, and cultural formations. IAM is a place of experimentation to see whether such a movement of changed perceptions can be implemented in a photographer's studio, at an artist's easel, from a theater stage. So as we journey forward, I urge you to journey with us. If anything in this book has stirred your heart, please begin to apply the principles in your life and your art, and let us know what happens.

Remember: our failure to think and act generatively, and our awareness of that failure, is the first step toward generativity. A culture care gathering may simply, at first, look like a group of people admitting that we fail to be generative but willing to ask for input from each other. Becoming generative is a constant principle and a continuing process. We need to acknowledge that we, in ourselves, may not have the power to regenerate what is decomposing in front of us or to push back against a culture that is dying. But by making this the starting point we may tap into what Wendell Berry calls the gift of the land, the gift of culture.

May our work be seeds into the soil of culture. Better yet, may these conversations strengthen our hands to cultivate that soil so that the good seed can take root deeply and flourish. May our cultural garden, our cultural orchard, become a place of shelter for many creatures, including our own grandchildren. May we stalk the borders and margins, accepting our deputized call to carry good news to the poor.

~ ~ ~

Let me finally answer the question I raised in the beginning of this introduction to culture care: Do we *need* beauty in our lives? If we desire to be fully human, the answer is yes, absolutely.

But we can now see, following the flow of thoughts so far, that even this question is ultimately utilitarian. We must shift from asking, What do we need? to What do we long for?

The biblical vision for the flourishing of our lives, lived fully under God's love, includes the beautiful. This is what we long for. What about you? What do you long for? Can beauty point to that reality? How you live out the answer to these questions is up to you. But the pursuit of these questions will lead to the feeding of our souls.

19

WHAT IF?

*W*hat if each of us endeavored to bring beauty into someone's life today in some small way?

What if we, by faith, saw each moment as a genesis moment, and even saw the current problems we are facing as genesis opportunities?

What if, instead of treating the independence and creativity of artists as problems to solve, we found in them opportunities for a new type of leadership in our current cultural flux?

What if artists became known for their generosity rather than only their self-expression?

What if art school became a place to train culture care agents rather than a filter that lets through only artists who can "make it"?

What if we considered our actions, decisions, and creative products in light of five hundred years and multiple generations?

What if we started to transgress boundaries by integrating our faith, art, and life—and speaking boldly about them?

What if we committed to speaking fresh creativity and vision into culture rather than denouncing and boycotting other cultural products?

What if we saw art as gift, not just as commodity?

What if we empower the border-stalkers in our communities, support them, and send them out?

What if we, like Mahalia Jackson, stood behind our preachers and leaders and exhorted them to "tell 'em about the dream"?

What if we created songs to draw people into movements for justice and flourishing?

What if we made things in secret, like Emily Dickinson, knowing that the world may not yet be ready for our thoughts?

What if we became custodians of culture, willing to be demoted for standing up for what is right but taking copious notes so we can challenge the status quo?

What if we assumed that relational and creative capital is infinite? What kind of effect would that have on our business practices?

What if we "gifted" photographs to share the light of the miraculous in people rather than "taking" photographs so that we can own and sell them?

YOUR "WHAT IFS"

Note down your own *what if* statements and share them with friends. Consider ways you can use these statements to help birth a plan for your community.

A GRATUITOUS POSTSCRIPT

Golden Sea was the result of a gratuitous act of creativity. While working intensely and semi-sequestered on the year-and-a-half project of *The Four Holy Gospels*, I needed a reprieve from the detail work of 140 pages of small illuminations. So I took a large canvas, stretched Kumohada paper over it, and began to work on it without any purpose for the piece. No exhibit awaited it, and I had not even a theme. It was a playground for my intuition, a gift to allow for materials to be layered and my soul to be nurtured so that when I sat to work on the illuminations I could draw on that freedom of movement and expression.

The resulting painting, now called *Golden Sea*, has become one of the seminal works of my career. My son Ty was hired by Crossway, publisher of *The Four Holy Gospels*, to take videos for that project. When he came into the studio while I was working on the illuminations, he asked me, "Hey, what's that painting?" By then it included over sixty layers of minerals and applied gold. "I don't know," I said. "It's something I've been working on." He paused to look. "It has everything you've ever done in it."

About two weeks later Valerie Dillon, owner of Dillon Gallery in New York, which represents my works, came in to see the illuminations and made a similar observation. As we discussed our upcoming retrospective catalogue, she said, "Of course, that painting will be on the cover, right?"

Sometimes the best work comes out in the daily discipline of working, when you are least expecting it. It is gratuitous, and at first peripheral, but then it reveals the core of who you are, as your intuition knows what needs to be expressed even before your rational mind, or the market, does.

I advise young artists always to do some work in secret, whether it be paintings that you never intend to show or a poem that you do not have to send to a publisher. Art resists being limited to utilitarian career making. Our intuition seems to crave the fully human abundance of joy, which is connected to God's act of gratuitous creation. God does not need us to exist; we do not fulfill God's needs. We are created in love, and the cosmos abounds with the delight of the Creator who created for love and wonder—and gives us a role to play in extending both.

Start now, today, to place that secret work in your "Emily Dickinson desk." May your intuition be nourished by the gift you have been given.

May our lives, our faith, and our art reflect and extend that gratuitous love and wonder.

May we always be willing to present a bouquet of flowers, even to an artist—or a culture—who may not yet know that they desire beauty.

ACKNOWLEDGMENTS

Culture Care was initially funded as an International Arts Movement publication. I would like to thank Ann Smith for her care in the initial editing process, Peter Edman for his extensive editorial contributions, and Lindsay Kolk for her beautiful design of the original book. I am also grateful for Amy Jones and Mark Rodgers of Wedgwood Circle for their encouragement to publish the introductory booklet for culture care called *On Becoming Generative*, for the Deschamps printing team for printing the award-winning booklet, and for the many people who supported the Kickstarter campaign making the publication of this book possible. I also gratefully acknowledge the board and staff of International Arts Movement, past and present, for their modeling culture care values even before we named them, particularly Chris and Barbara Giammona for their support of the creation of this book. Amy Dwyer, Joe Gallegher, and many others have been critical in helping me to carve out time to work on this book. I am grateful for my new post at Brehm Center, under the vision of president Mark Labberton, to implement culture care values into Fuller Seminary education. Fujimura Institute brings culture care values into academia, and the Fujimura Fellows of Brehm|Fujimura Studios brings culture care into action in churches and in the world. I am excited about our future together.

I am also grateful for my wife and my children who are constant reminders of beauty to me.

DISCUSSION GUIDE

By Julie Silander and Peter Edman

ABOUT THIS GUIDE

The questions in this guide are designed to spark further personal reflection and group conversation on the topics related to culture care. Choose a facilitator to guide the conversation for your group. For each gathering, the facilitator should plan ahead and choose one or two chapters to discuss, then focus on two or three questions that seem most relevant to your circumstances and available time.

We hope that conversations on this book and topic will be generative and even surprising, so try to leave time to discuss related questions or topics that will arise naturally from your group. Keep a record of ideas your group generates or wants to act on, and come back to them in a few months to see how you are doing.

If the book and discussions start you on a creative journey, consider sharing this with us. Contact us at iamculturecare.com/contact. Or tag us on Twitter and Instagram: @IntlArtsMvmnt. International Arts Movement also has a website and a community group on Facebook.

PREFACE

- When have you worked to understand a viewpoint different from your own? What was that experience like? How are you different as a result?

- In a personal relationship, work environment, or collaborative effort, have you ever shifted from a posture of being braced to win to a posture of serving in love? What caused the change? What was the outcome?

1 ON BECOMING GENERATIVE

- The word *generative* is derived from a Latin word meaning "to beget." Judy, in bringing home flowers, birthed beauty in the home, which birthed a shift in perspective and heart, which birthed a growing movement that is still influencing families, churches, and communities. What stood out to you about this story of a generative act?

- Did any of the three Gs in this chapter surprise you? Would they have been familiar to people from past generations or other cultures?

- Have there been times when you have been jarred out of a cycle of worry by an act of beauty? What fed your soul or helped you to escape a survival mentality? Try to paint a picture with your words.

- Fujimura suggests that "something is awakened through failure, tragedy, and disappointment." What is awakened? What does "the hope of something new" after failure mean to you?

- Tell about a time when what began as failure eventually resulted in growth.

- Whose souls do you hope to feed? How? Remember, feeding a soul doesn't have to be a grand gesture—and rarely is.

- Think about people in your community and spheres of influence. How might each change by more encounters with generosity? What would it look like for you to be more generous toward these people—with your time, resources, story, and gifting? List a few examples.

- What are two or three factors that stand in the way of your being more generous? What steps can you take to bypass those obstacles? What does the author suggest is the benefit of encounters with generosity?

2 CULTURE CARE DEFINED

- Did you resonate with the definition of culture care as providing "care for our culture's 'soul'"?

- Andy Crouch has argued that a society's health can be measured by the degree that the most vulnerable are flourishing.[1] Who are the most vulnerable in your country? In your community? In your family?

- What would flourishing—a condition in which people are growing and thriving—look like for each of these vulnerable groups?

- Name a few current environmental concerns. What are people doing to address such current or potential problems? Could (and should) these approaches be translated to the cultural sphere—our social environment?

- List several adjectives that describe our culture. Do any describe a current or future threat to our society's health?

- Think of ways that people from different backgrounds contribute to the common good. What does it mean to be a person of good will in a fragmented culture?

- Fujimura summarizes culture care as "applied generative thinking." What does that statement mean to you?

3 BLACK RIVER, CRACKED LANDS

- Name a few of the communities to which you belong. Which is most influential in your life? In which do you have influence?

- Fujimura writes, "Sometimes we are more aware of our dependence and sometimes we are more aware of our contributions, but we exist in community." Think of people who seem more dependent. What does their presence offer to the community?

- For each of the communities you listed, what influences threaten harmony and thriving? A few examples might be external media; family, regional, or national history; or educational disparity. It's not an easy question to answer, but it's an important one. Consider making a list of cultural pollutants, and add to it over several days.

- Can you think of specific technological or financial successes that have contributed to cultural fragmentation? How does the background assumption that efficiency equates with progress play out in your faith community, neighborhood, workplace, family, or friendships?

- How might each of these social relationships be different if efficiency were devalued? Can you imagine a slower pace of life? Can you think of ways to make more margin in your life?

- Have you experienced hyperspecialization and over-reliance on experts? Does anyone have a broad knowledge of all the many roles and responsibilities in your life?

- Who is accountable for ethical and humane activity in medicine, education, or government? What other segments of society come to mind? Name one way that people would benefit if each of these spheres were made less fragmented.

- How has the drive toward efficiency and hyperspecialization manifested in the world of art? Have you seen the trajectory that

Fujimura identifies in the arts toward commercialization and ideological exploitation?

- Why does the gap between artists and the wider society matter?

4 FROM CULTURE WARS TO A COMMON LIFE

- Name an issue that is prominent in our culture wars. What could another voice that chooses to steward rather than to win speak into the conversation?

- Fujimura says, "Culture is not a territory to be won or lost but a resource we are called to steward with care." Think about how environmental stewardship works. What are some models that could transfer to supporting creativity and community?

- How could generosity inform conversations with current culture-war combatants?

- What is the appeal of choosing opposition rather than sharing? What would the shift toward sharing require? How could art help facilitate such a shift?

- The author reminds us that "destruction and dissolution are far easier than creation and connection." What character traits are called for in those who are working for cultural cultivation and regeneration?

5 SOUL CARE

- Name three cultural problems in your country, your city, or your neighborhood. What do you think is a fundamental longing underlying each problem?

- Can you identify people who are culturally self-aware and can see human longings beneath the issues we face? What do these people contribute to the conversation? How could you help them or emulate them? If you cannot identify anyone like this, can you think of ways you could encourage others to look for these deeper questions?

- Describe a time when identifying and naming brokenness in your own life moved you toward beauty, wholeness, or healing.

- When was the last time you had training or apprenticeship (formal or informal) related to seeing beauty more deeply? What was it?

- What area of aesthetic experience would you like to explore more deeply? What could a first step be? Consider reading a book, taking a class, attending a lecture or performance, or even having coffee with someone who could help you grow in that direction.

6 BEAUTY AS FOOD FOR THE SOUL

- What images came to mind as you read the working definition of beauty in this chapter? What is your earliest memory of experiencing something that was a delight to the senses, a pleasure to the mind, and a refreshment for the spirit? Paint a picture with your words.

- How would you explain the difference between survival and flourishing?

- Have you considered the act of creating more (gratuitous) beauty as one of stewardship? As a divine request? If so, how has that belief shaped your actions? If not, think how your gifting, skills, and resources might be used to create beauty.

- This chapter quotes the philosopher Elaine Scarry as saying, "Beauty, sooner or later, brings us into contact with our own capacity for making errors." What do you make of that statement?

- How would you explain the connection between justice and beauty?

7 LEADERSHIP FROM THE MARGINS

- Have you felt as if you exist on the edges of a group? Do you know people who do? Did the concept of the *mearcstapa* help you or give you ideas about how to contribute to your society?

- Summarize the value of border-stalkers. What are some of the dangers such a role would bring?

- How can artists be border-stalkers for our culture?

- Do you think artists are able to see the common humanity in the "other"? If so, where does that ability come from? What can we learn from their example?

- Have you encountered people who are adaptable in their cultural expression but committed to a set of core convictions? How do they react to new circumstances?

- Which is more lacking in our current culture—adaptability or holding to core beliefs? What is more lacking in the church?

8 "TELL 'EM ABOUT THE DREAM!"

- The author discusses Harper Lee's *To Kill a Mockingbird* (and elsewhere, Tolkien's *Lord of the Rings*). Can you think of other books, films, plays, or songs that have shifted or shaped the culture in which they were created?

- Think about news headlines from the past two or three weeks. What person or group might be an "other" or a scapegoat in to-day's culture? In the case you named, what is the core fear that feeds the drive for "justice"? What would it look like in this situation to take a small step away from fear and toward acknowl-edging our common humanity? Think of a way that you could take a first small step.

- Name a few people who were formative in your thinking about social responsibility.

- The author suggests that those who would be reconcilers in culture "must speak like children," which includes being "innocent of pre-tense and full of determined hope." What other themes does he draw out of childlikeness? Have you seen people who display these characteristics? What are roadblocks to these ideals?

- Why does a call for justice need to be presented beautifully?

9 TWO LIVES AT THE MARGINS

- Were you challenged or comforted by any of the themes highlighted in these stories of two lives?

- What did relationship with the church look like for Emily Dickinson and Vincent van Gogh? How do you think the church viewed each of them?

- What do you think is the church's relationship to artists today? Why?

10 OUR CALLING IN THE STARRY NIGHT

- The author says, "Our calling, simply as humans—and more so as followers of Christ—is wider than our career and our survival, even in the modern age." List four or five nouns that represent various aspects of your calling. Which ones fall outside the categories of *career* or *survival*?

- Have you seen cases where people who are not "useful" are exiled from the "normal" world? In those cases, has anyone been able to see past the marginalized people's utility to their full humanity? What happened? Give examples.

- Fujimura says that "art is ultimately not 'useful.' It serves no practical function." Do you agree? Why or why not? Why would this make art indispensable?

- What is the difference between being a "Christian artist" (or other noun of your choice) and a "Christian who is an artist"? Why does Fujimura suggest that this difference is important? Where do you commonly see *Christian* being used as an adjective rather than a noun? Are any of those examples problematic?

- How do the arts help bridge the gap between *thriving* and *surviving*?

11 OPENING THE GATES

- Have you seen churches create rigid boundaries with high barriers and closed gates? Are there cases where that is appropriate? Have you encountered situations where a rigid boundary might indicate a lack of trust in the Good Shepherd?

- Would you describe your upbringing as (1) shut inside the pen, (2) sheltered inside the pen and free to graze in green pastures, or (3) outside the gate?

- Which of the three would describe your parenting philosophy?

- Which of the three best describes your church?

- Do you currently have places outside a safe pen where you find green grass—and encounter Jesus' "other sheep," those who are "not of this sheep pen"? Have you recognized the work of the Holy Spirit in such potentially uncomfortable settings?

- What are some ways we hold our gates shut? What would have to change to have open gates? What would it look like for the church to be a place of homecoming and welcome (for the good of the sheep within as well as those outside)?

- How does the author describe a healthy community? Have you seen or been a part of such a community? What are a few adjectives that would best describe it? How has it blessed the wider world?

12 CULTIVATING CULTURAL SOIL

- When we think of culture as soil, what activities are our responsibility, and what must be left to time or to God? What does Fujimura suggest are "seeds"?

- How have artifacts (tangible pieces of culture such as art, music, or literature) of earlier cultures contributed to the nourishment of new seeds in our culture? Give an example or two.

- How do you respond to the reminder that we live under a command to participate in God's creative work? What are your spheres of influence? For each, what are some practical ways that you can participate in God's creative purposes, extend his artistry, and contribute to the transformation of disorder?

- How does culture care prepare the way for the gospel to be spread?

- What does it look like to have healthy cultural soil? Name a few indicators.

- Why is the author calling for a long-term, community-level, nurturing approach to culture? What does he foresee growing from properly channeled human gifting?

- What does Fujimura see as the drawbacks of a "greenhouse" approach to cultivation?

13 CULTURAL ESTUARIES

- Fujimura says that estuaries are focused less on *protection* and more on *preparation*. How could this model apply to friendship? Parenting? Church?

- Do you find the estuary model clarifying or confusing? Are you or artists you know more like oysters or salmon, or something else entirely?

- The author briefly mentions several historical examples of the estuary concept. Are you familiar with any of them? Can you draw any lessons from them that may apply to your current context?

- Explain the five steps that Fujimura lists to provide practical support so that artists are more likely to be generative than transgressive:

"We can deputize them, then form, train, commission, and support them." Which of these is most lived out in your community? What does that look like?

- Considering your resources, time, and gifts, where do you see yourself most likely stepping in to become a part of (or more deeply involved in) the process of supporting artists?

14 CUSTODIANS OF CULTURE CARE

- The author says that culture care requires sacrifice. What does sacrifice look like for you?

- What is your earliest memory of being connected to or moved by art, music, dance, theater, or story? Take a few minutes to share the scene in detail.

- Fujimura suggests that the measurement of success is generational, not in efficiency. How can we sustain our efforts over such a long time frame? Are these metrics inherently in conflict? Why or why not?

- What would culture care manifesting itself in the lives of our children look like?

15 BUSINESS CARE

- Can you think of two or three creative catalysts from your community? Describe their involvement in caring for the culture.

- Name barriers to the formation of a union between the business world and creative people. What is one step that could help overcome those barriers?

- How could you invite business people into such a discussion?

- The chapter includes a graphic illustrating "rehumanized capitalism," which suggests that any movement needs three kinds of capital. In your community, which of these three elements is strongest? Weakest? How might you strengthen the weakest element?

- What is the difference between *sustainable* and *generative*?

16 PRACTICAL ADVICE FOR ARTISTS

- How does Fujimura distinguish between survival mode and a generative path when artists are struggling to make a living?

- What are the practical implications of investing resources (time, money, gifting) in creating ripple effects that may last five hundred years rather than into immediate experience? What would be the litmus test for your investments?

- When have you experienced closed doors along the path toward your calling? How would you describe your posture when facing those challenges? Have you been able to maintain an outlook that is positive enough for you to persevere through adversity?

- Do you resonate with the distinction made between an "easy path" and an "abundant path"?

17 TILLING OUR CULTURAL SOIL IN THE AGE OF ANXIETY

- Do you agree that culture care can actually save lives? How might it do so in your context?

- What is the difference between "common ground" and "common life"?

- What examples do you know of people working together for the sake of common life despite marked differences?

- The author states that, like bees, "artists have a reputation of being hard to deal with and even toxic to the group" and are often isolated from communities. Have you seen this happening? What are the effects for the artists and the communities?

- How could art and artists be more integrated into the realities of life for all people instead of being sequestered and elitist?

18 NEW VOCABULARIES, NEW STORIES

- Do you have a group that can become a cultural estuary, a microcosm of care?

- Think about conversations you've had over the past year. Did you participate in a culture-war battle or use the vocabulary of culture wars? How might you approach a similar conversation after spending time with culture care principles?

- As you've read through the book, what principle has affected you most? What thoughts or ideas have been stirred?

- What do you long for in your life? In your community? Church? Workplace?

- What relationship does beauty have to those longings?

19 WHAT IF?

- Choose three or four questions from the list and respond to them. Write in a journal. Sketch a picture. Create something tangible that will mark this point along your journey.

A GRATUITOUS POSTSCRIPT

- Consider some of the stories from the author's life mentioned in this book. He works in community and is arguing for a public role for art, but here he speaks about work done alone and in secret. Is there a connection between secret work and the soul care concept introduced earlier?

- Have you thought about "creating in secret"? What value could you see in doing so? Whether or not you are a practicing artist, think about what you can begin to make in secret that would participate in and extend God's gratuitous creativity. What steps will you take? What sacrifices should you make?

NOTES

2 CULTURE CARE DEFINED

[1]See Noam Chomsky, *On Language* (New York: New Press, 2007).

3 BLACK RIVER, CRACKED LANDS

[1]I write about this episode in the essay "Refractions 24: The Resonance of Being," June 14, 2007, www.makotofujimura.com/writings/refractions-24-the-resonance-of-being.

[2]Thank you, Nigel Goodwin, for the "Nigelisms" that continue to encourage us. He often finishes the phrase, "and we are human becomings."

[3]See Robert Hughes, *The Shock of the New* (New York: McGraw Hill, 2009).

4 FROM CULTURE WARS TO A COMMON LIFE

[1]James Davison Hunter, *Culture Wars: The Struggle to Define America* (New York: Basic Books, 1991), 325.

[2]Listen, for example, to an interview with artist Dario Robleto: "Dario Robleto—Sculptor of Memory," *On Being*, hosted by Krista Tippett, July 24, 2014, www.onbeing.org/program/dario-robleto-sculptor-of-memory/6640.

[3]T. S. Eliot, *Notes Towards the Definition of Culture* (New York: Harcourt, Brace and Company, 1949), 26.

5 SOUL CARE

[1]Erwin Raphael McManus, *The Artisan Soul* (New York: HarperOne, 2014), 33-34.

[2]Wesley Hill, commenting on a post at wesleyhill.tumblr.com, July 10, 2014.

6 BEAUTY AS FOOD FOR THE SOUL

[1]Quoted in John Ortberg, "Dallas Willard, a Man from Another 'Time Zone,'" *Christianity Today*, May 8, 2013, www.christianitytoday.com/ct/2013/may-web-only/man-from-another-time-zone.html.

[2]Roger Scruton, lecture (University Club, Washington, DC, December 1, 2009).

[3]J. R. R. Tolkien, "On Fairy Stories," in *The Tolkien Reader* (New York: Ballantine Books, 1966), 58.

[4]Elaine Scarry, *On Beauty and Being Just* (Princeton, NJ: Princeton University Press, 1999), 31, 35.

7 LEADERSHIP FROM THE MARGINS

[1]*Mearcstapa* is one of several terms used to describe Grendel. See the Mearcstapa organization website, www.mearcstapa.org. A helpful essay is Erica Weaver, "*Beowulf* and the Anglo-Saxon Mark: Borders, Transgression, and Grendel's Arm" (conference paper, New England Medieval Studies Consortium Graduate Student Conference, Brown University, March 2011), published in *Sententiae: The Harvard Undergraduate Journal of Medieval Studies*, June 2, 2011.

[2]J. R. R. Tolkien, *The Lord of the Rings: The Fellowship of the Ring* (New York: Ballantine, 1973), 232.

8 "TELL 'EM ABOUT THE DREAM!"

[1]Harper Lee, *To Kill a Mockingbird* (New York: HarperCollins, 2002), 39.

[2]Ibid., 6.

[3]Ibid, 205.

[4]Ibid.

[5]Many Christians respond similarly to cultural artifacts, focusing on surface offenses rather than going deep enough to see truths.

[6]Scout also reminds us of the difficulty of true nonviolence when she kicks a man in the shin for trying to remove Jem from the scene.

[7]Clarence Benjamin Jones, "On Martin Luther King Day, Remembering the First Draft of 'I Have a Dream,'" *The Washington Post*, January 16, 2011, www.washingtonpost.com/wp-dyn/content/article/2011/01/14/AR2011011406266.html.

[8]Howard E. Gardner, *Intelligence Reframed: Multiple Intelligences for the 21st Century* (New York: Basic Books, 2000), 130-49.

[9]Quoted in Alden Whitman, "Mahalia Jackson, Gospel Singer and a Civil Rights Symbol, Dies," *New York Times*, January 28, 1972.

9 TWO LIVES AT THE MARGINS

[1]This chapter includes material adapted from "Refractions 36: 'The Hyphen

of the Sea"—A Journey with Emily Dickinson (Part 1)," May 25, 2011, www .makotofujimura.com/writings/refractions-36-the-hyphen-of-the-sea-a -journey-with-emily-dickinson-part-1.

[2]Emily Dickinson, *The Poems of Emily Dickinson: Reading Edition*, ed. Ralph W. Franklin (Cambridge, MA: The Belknap Press of Harvard University Press, 1951).

[3]See the book of Ezekiel, especially chapters 1, 3, 10, and 11.

[4]Sydney R. McLean, "Emily Dickinson at Mount Holyoke," *The New England Quarterly* 7, no. 1 (1934): 25-42.

[5]Roger Lundin, *Emily Dickinson and the Art of Belief*, Library of Religious Biography (Grand Rapids: Eerdmans, 1998), 53.

[6]Letter #164, from Vincent van Gogh to Theo van Gogh, c. December 21, 1881. See http://vangoghletters.org.

[7]Quoted in Fritz Erpel, *Van Gogh: The Self-Portraits* (New York: New York Graphic Society, 1969), 17.

[8]This section and portions of the following chapter are adapted from my 2012 commencement address to the graduate school at Biola University. The full text can be found at "'The Starry Night': Biola University Commencement Address, May, 2012," May 26, 2012, www.makotofujimura.com/writings /the-starry-night-biola-university-commencement-address-may-2012.

[9]Letter B8, from Vincent van Gogh to Émile Bernard, June 23, 1888; in *Vincent van Gogh: Painted with Words* (New York: Rizzoli, 2007), 190-92.

10 OUR CALLING IN THE STARRY NIGHT

[1]Dana Gioia, commencement address (Stanford University, Stanford, CA, June 18, 2007).

11 OPENING THE GATES

[1]I am grateful for the journey that C.J. has led to teach me of the *mearcstapa* role. This chapter is a gift from him to the reader, with his permission.

[2]This section is adapted from material originally published in Makoto Fujimura, "Artist in Residence Series: Culture Care for Churches," *Transpositions*, the blog of the Institute for Theology, Imagination and the Arts at the University of St. Andrews, March 26, 2014, www.transpositions.co.uk/culture -care-for-churches.

[3]Thanks to Gordon Pennington for this observation.

12 CULTIVATING CULTURAL SOIL

[1]Christian Wiman, "Varieties of Quiet," *Image* 73 (2012), https://imagejournal
.org/article/varieties-of-quiet.

[2]Wendell Berry, "The Gift of Good Land," *Flourish Magazine*, Fall 2009,
www.flourishonline.org/2011/04/wendell-berry-gift-of-good-land.

[3]Lewis Hyde, *The Gift: Creativity and the Artist in the Modern World*, 2nd ed.
(New York: Vintage, 2007), xvi.

14 CUSTODIANS OF CULTURE CARE

[1]From the transcript of *America's First River: Bill Moyers on the Hudson*, Part 2,
PBS/Public Affairs Television, Inc., 2002, www-tc.pbs.org/now/science
/HUDSON2.pdf.

17 TILLING OUR CULTURAL SOIL
IN THE AGE OF ANXIETY

[1]Reinhold Niebuhr, *Major Works on Religion and Politics*, Kindle ed. (New York:
Library of America, 2015), loc. 6358.

[2]Reinhold Niebuhr, *The Irony of American History* (1952; repr., Chicago: University of Chicago Press, 2008), 63.

[3]Martin Luther King Jr., "I've Been to the Mountaintop" (speech at Mason
Temple, Memphis, Tennessee, April 3, 1968); available at American Rhetoric,
www.americanrhetoric.com/speeches/mlkivebeentothemountaintop.htm.

[4]W. H. Vanstone, *Love's Endeavour, Love's Expense: The Response of Being to the
Love of God* (London: Darton, Longman and Todd, 1977), 34.

DISCUSSION GUIDE

[1]See Andy Crouch, *Strong and Weak: Embracing a Life of Love, Risk and True
Flourishing* (Downers Grove, IL: InterVarsity Press, 2016).

ABOUT THE AUTHOR

Makoto Fujimura is an internationally renowned artist, writer, and speaker who serves as the director of Fuller Theological Seminary's Brehm Center for Worship, Theology, and the Arts. He is also the founder of the International Arts Movement and served as a presidential appointee to the National Council on the Arts from 2003 to 2009. His books include *Refractions: A Journey of Faith, Art and Culture, Silence and Beauty,* and *Culture Care.*

Recognized worldwide as a cultural shaper, Fujimura has had work exhibited at galleries including Dillon Gallery in New York, Sato Museum in Tokyo, The Contemporary Museum of Tokyo, Tokyo National University of Fine Arts Museum, Bentley Gallery in Arizona, Taikoo Place in Hong Kong, and Vienna's Belvedere Museum. In 2011 the Fujimura Institute was established and launched the Qu4rtets, a collaboration between Fujimura, painter Bruce Herman, Duke theologian/pianist Jeremy Begbie, and Yale composer Christopher Theofanidis, based on T. S. Eliot's *Four Quartets.*

A popular speaker, Fujimura has lectured at numerous conferences, universities, and museums, including the Aspen Institute, Yale and Princeton Universities, Sato Museum, and the Phoenix Art Museum. Among many awards and recognitions, Bucknell University honored him with the Outstanding Alumni Award in

2012, and the American Academy of Religion named him as its 2014 Religion and the Arts award recipient. He has received honorary doctorates from Belhaven University, Biola University, Cairn University, and Roanoke College.

ALSO BY MAKOTO FUJIMURA

Silence and Beauty:
Hidden Faith Born of Suffering
978-0-8308-4459-3